Plank Conversations

A Handbook of Hope You Exercise Your Right to Vote

by:
Mark Clemons

DORRANCE
PUBLISHING CO
EST. 1920
PITTSBURGH, PENNSYLVANIA 15238

Dorrance Publishing Co
585 Alpha Drive
Pittsburgh, PA 15238
Visit our website at www.dorrancebookstore.com

ISBN: 978-1-6491-3767-8
eISBN: 978-1-6491-3955-9

For young adults and the young at heart,

for embracing a better future

Dedicated to my daughter, who has

embraced always voting

Table of Contents

Introduction by the Author

First off, you must know that I have no desire for elective office. I am retired. Writing is an outlet. Sure, there may be others who kicked off successful political careers after having written a book or two. This is not for me. I'm too old to hold down an overtime gig like that. I receive a pension now from having worked nearly thirty years in a hospital/medical system. There were other jobs on my resume, and I'm done with them, too. Also, I'm writing under a pen name in an attempt to maintain some semblance of a private life, so don't expect to see me out campaigning for office.

Why write this book? I have noted there are many a millennial and other younger voting age folks out there who feel the American Dream of a home and the pursuit of happiness have been stripped away from them and their peers. Wage inequity will do that to a generation that can't afford the escalating cost of owning a home. Don't give up the Dream! We have some obstacles in our way, but we can get this turned around for the better.

Some of the younger disaffected complain that the constitutional framers failed to get it right the first time. It was intended to be a Living Document, subject to change. Some of those framers had slaves which the youth of today can rightly claim them to have been quite barbarous.

Be glad you didn't live then but bear in mind we will be considered the barbarous ancestors a hundred years from now.

Democracy is not a spectator sport. Voting is the one and only way to make a better democracy. Vote every time, as if your life depended upon it. It does. Just because your favorite choice isn't on the ballot doesn't mean you should skip voting. Get a vote club together. The more who vote, the greater the likelihood that there will be better outcomes. You may not always win, but you will have earned the right to gripe about the results!

For the older electorate, the same old, same old just won't cut it anymore. Fresh ideas need to be presented to invigorate the younger population. Being a Centrist in the hopes of getting the broad spectrum of people to vote for a candidate will lead only to the same road to nowhere. Moderation in moderation must be the new standard. Let's make a breakthrough!

Also, you must have hope. The country that elected Barack Obama still exists. People must get out to vote to affect change. If you're not voting, you can't complain about the results. Voting is the single most important thing we do. Participate in hope, by voting.

We really can make a difference. Currently there are forces out there trying to dilute or eliminate voter participation. We, The People, must vote to prevent that. Fresh ideas and open discussion without calling each other names would help. Be the change, get more people to vote, step out and believe we can move this plodding force of inertia. We CAN do this.

The ideas here are conversational talking points. Moving forward is our means to an end. It isn't expected that all things presented here will be completely agreed with by one and all, but the topics need to be moved on. We, the 99 percent, must speak with our votes and while we still can vote. We may not have the power of money, but we have the power of numbers. Let's use it.

It is my intent to interject a little humor along the way, despite the seriousness of the subject matter. Some will laugh, others might say, "Hey! I resemble that remark!" I can make some of the people laugh some of the time, but I know I can't make all of the people laugh all of the time.

Finally, if some of these Ideas gain a little traction and I've written the fifth book of a trilogy with movie rights, I would, at the behest of a clamoring force, be willing to take on the title of Grand Pooh-Bah, Excellency of Terra Firma. No elective office, however. I've got too many other things to do or put off already. I'm swamped.

PS – I took my pen name in honor of a well-known American author and Abolitionist.

PPS – Should these Ideas come to be leaked out upon the world-at-large, please feel free to change the name of the country or locality mentioned here-in, to include your own favorite. Some of us beg for Universal Change.

1. "I don't belong to any organized political faith; I
    am a Democrat." Will Rogers, Quote from *Will
    Rogers: A Political Life* by Richard D. White Jr.

Interesting how time passes yet things remain the same. It's been over ninety years since that quote and still the Democrats are as organized and united as ever—no resemblance to a cohesive unit. They could just as easily stake out a platform simply stating, "We are not Republicans!" and leave it at that. Though this would be enough for many of the voting population, the rest need a little more to hang their hat on. I'm hoping to help the Democratic powers focus up the message a bit, with some humor thrown in just to keep a smile on my face and hopefully yours, too.

First off, I'd like to discuss Democracy. In the nearly 250 years since the people of the United States began this stunning and unique government there have been any number of complaints about how the government was formed and the hypocrisies of the many famous members of this institution. They did mean well. In the end analysis, any problem in Democracy can be readily attributed to it's being run by humans, as we are inherently flawed. We are the they that holds us back from perfection. Democracy will, in the long run though, give the best chance for all.

Great words infuse the Constitution and Declaration of Independence. We must continue to honor the good intentions of those who fought to throw off monarchy and the privilege and hierarchies of feudal lords. I look back and admire how tenaciously and long they struggled to make this dream come true. It is at our own peril to forget the sacrifices that were made to create and keep this truly tremendous Union.

Democracy is a participation sport. For Democracy to work best, people need to exercise their right to vote. Voter turnout should always be better than 85 percent. There are those who would wish to make it harder to vote. Don't let them win. Get out and participate in Democracy. You don't have to join marches to make a difference, though that may help. Vote! Voting is the most important thing we ever do for ourselves. It does make a difference—never again should you believe some poll that someone who is expected to win will actually get the votes to win. Participate and vote to make it happen!

Currently, there are forces at work who would suppress the voters who don't tow their line. They gerrymander districts to create unequal majorities. These are the same folks who don't want to pay for anything but are willing to borrow money to give more to those who already have it. By promoting trickle-down theory, feudalism returns. The old money grabs for what it can to grow their piece of the pie. They don't want their fiefdoms to slip away.

Fortunately, the voting public don't believe making our children and grandchildren pay for today's government is fiscally responsible. Sure, "Less taxes!" sounds great, but the piper must be paid at some point. We need to pay for our bills now, not expect our children and theirs to pony up. "Less taxes!" and "Less government!" is a recipe for letting the rich control the country. It isn't fiscal responsibility. Let's move toward letting our children and grandchildren pay for their own mistakes, not ours!

Democracy. It really is the best form of government. It may not be perfect, but that's only because it's run by us, mere humans. Many young people are saying their parent's generation made this country so messed up. Not true, it was my parent's generation. Kidding aside, it's been a long road, and everyone is to blame. We can make it better and that comes from participation. Apathy is the tool used by those who would prefer to tell you how to live and apathy has allowed fiscal irresponsibility to grow. Do not allow that to continue. Join in, try to make a difference, and get out to vote! Voting works; in numbers there is strength! Ninety-nine percenters can make it work better.

The Democrats need guidance and a simple message to be identified with. In 1992 the candidate with the KISS policy was able to win the election. Keep It Simply Simple—don't complicate the message. People do care about living wage jobs, affordable housing, social security solvency, reducing the federal deficit, healthcare, education, and keeping their family safe. A simple platform they can identify with and is easy to understand works best. Politics has gotten to the extreme where yelling and screaming substitutes for substance. With luck, voters have had enough of it and more people will start voting. Democracy works best when everyone participates.

The large family I hail from includes the type that felt the louder they yelled, the more correct their position was. You may have them in your family, too. ENOUGH! By and large, the bulk of the current crop of yellers and screamers believe that "the only way to make a better country is to choke the government of funds to make it (the government) so small that it can just go away since private enterprise will always make life better for everyone by doing things more efficiently." We can be certain they must also believe in the Tooth Fairy. If you've ever watched the movie Gangs of New York and seen the rival fire departments at work, you might think twice about putting your full faith into letting private enterprise control your life.

The faith anti-government folk have that private enterprise has the answer to all questions boils down to their true and simple religious belief, "No taxes, No government." There are places where they can go to enjoy this type system, and I invite them to leave immediately for Somalia, or Greece, so they can experience the system and live it. Really, please go. Let the rest of us live in a country where things are a little more complex and take work and money to get things done. I don't like to call anyone names but the sort of person who can't look past their own pocketbook makes me think of the seagulls in the movie Finding Nemo, always yelling, "Mine, mine, mine!"

Much as it would be nice to believe large corporations and the well-to-do 1 percent who control the majority of wealth in the country and world will do things in the best interest of all, it won't happen if they're making the decisions. One thing I appreciate about government is that you can vote for the people running it. When was the last time you got to vote for the president of your bank, insurance company, or energy corporation? Or how much they were to be paid? We would be told we could do that if we bought shares. Of course, our possible few shares wouldn't carry much weight against those holding a million shares—they can buy the election!

What we do have is Democracy, and I'd like to keep it, where everyone has an equal vote, and all get represented. Ideally. There are plenty of people who "don't trust the government." There will always be people who take advantage of their positions in high places, whether it's government or business; that is human nature. We are in no danger of suppressing human nature. With Democracy, we have a chance to put the people in place to make things work correctly. We won't get that chance if corporations run things on their whims. Who do you trust more, the Government or Business? Of course, the answer is neither, but at least with government you have a voice. This is truly a precious thing, being able to vote. More people should try it; we'd all be better off!

Unfortunately, the religious fervor of the "No Taxes, No Government" cult would prefer to create their view of Utopia for us and borrow our way to Greece's state of financial instability. In the religion I grew up in, we knew we had to pay for our sins, instead of making your children, grandchildren, and great-grandchildren pay for them. Like the whipping boys of British royalty. Benjamin Franklin said, "There is nothing certain but death and taxes." If we want to have roads, healthcare, good jobs, personal and financial security in our retirement, we will have to pay taxes. To keep our debt from dominating the government budget, we must consider giving the rich an opportunity to pay a greater percentage of their income so we can reduce that debt. How many Rolexes do they need?

If not now, when? The "Mine! Mine! Mine!" group will always contend we're in crisis and that the economy will collapse if we tax the poor rich folk. A fellow worker with me for the last thirty years is one of them. I think of him as a brother but can't fathom his thought that these poor rich folk have already done their fair share. We who get the actual work done are down here sweating while the movers and shakers are smoking their cigars, drinking scotch, trying to think up ways to wring more money from the rest of us. The fact there is wealth inequity has become more and more apparent; even (gasp) Republicans allowed the expression to escape their lips during the 2016 campaign, though, not since. How then can we start to right the ship and raise the tide? Not by borrowing money to give to those who already have it.

Our forebears wrote the laws to try to ensure we would not go back to the system of hereditary lords running our lives. There does seem to be an air of privilege that comes naturally to many of the 1 percent. Royalty and rank—and I do mean rank; the rank of privilege stinks. We don't need a House of Lords to run our lives. In the White House now resides He Who Would Be King. Given the opportunity, these would-be-lords would like us to return to serfdom and just do what we're told. Don't let them.

Remember the sacrifices made by the revolutionaries who created a country where we can all be equals. It was a new concept. They made it work despite the many differences in opinion in how to go about it. It made us a country that people all over the world wanted to come to or duplicate in their own homelands. We the people. Powerful words. Believe in them. Vote to make a difference, because that is where the power is.

Sure, "All men are created equal" didn't initially apply to slaves, or women. Eventually it did. It is still a work in progress. It will always be. There are those who would limit who gets to vote. Things will only get better if more people participate by voting. If you think "My vote won't make a difference," you've already let "them" win. Encourage your neighbors and friends. Together we can make it better. Voting twice a year is not a colonoscopy. Just vote. Consider it a duty to yourself, family, your friends and neighbors and fellow country people. Participating will make things better. Please do not let the efforts of those who have died to make and hold on to this unique standard go to waste.

The base of The Statue of Liberty has powerful words written on it. Donald the First would rather put a tarp over those words, probably the whole statue. Let us not forget we are mostly descendants from migrants who came here for a better life. That is what the great majority of those who still come here want, a better life. Few of them are here to take our jobs or rape and pillage, but they will do the jobs that those of us born here have no desire to do. Face it, they need to keep coming in to fill the jobs Americans don't want.

The jobs that need creation are for infrastructure improvement and maintenance. There will never be enough people to do all those jobs. We will have to pay for them, though. Private enterprise won't get it done. None of us want to be on that bridge or overpass that falls. We must pay for it one way or the other. We'll never get around to taking care of it all as long as the government operates on deficit spending, borrowing to give to those whom already possess it. That's Socialism for the Privileged.

The Republican Party has been hijacked by people who want future generations to pay for their lifestyles. Why do they hate their children so much that they would burden them with their bills? That is a great question. Since the Bush Recession ended, the economy has been on the continued upswing for many years. When will we start to pay our bills? A good time is when the economy thrives. Let's vote for fiscal responsibility.

The Democrats must evolve to spark the emotion in the young voters. The message must be clear, simple, and speak to the inequities which are looming in the young person's life. Life, liberty, and the pursuit of happiness appear out of reach with soaring house prices, student loans, and lack of suitable job prospects. Let's get them on board to bridge the inequities they see and help them realize there is hope in the future, because there is hope.

There is a lot of work to do. Every epic journey begins with the first step. There will be trials and tribulations ahead, but that goes without saying. In this New Age of Misinformation, it becomes more difficult to get people to agree on anything. The internet serves as a place of truth and lies that make it difficult to tell the difference between. Bridging that gap is paramount.

New leaders need to focus up their presentation and simplify their platform then keep repeating it. That's how He Who Would Be King won the election. In the final days of the campaign any question put to him was answered with one of five pat sayings. Usually these quips had with nothing to do with the question.

I've got six things the Democrats can start with. It is just a start, but you must begin somewhere. The actual list is a bit longer, and I'll cover a few. In the meantime, the internet's explosion of Misinformation will have to be tempered with a supernova of facts. The web has a confusion of authors with any number of made up beliefs. It's time to get real facts into the world-at-large and cyberspace. Infused, of course, with a few cat or dog videos.

2. "I'll believe corporations are people when Texas
    executes one of them." Attributed to Flickr—and
    we thank you very much!

First and foremost, we must repeal the Citizens United decision which allowed that corporations, under their first amendment rights(?), can spend as much money as they want to promote their political views. I still recall George W. saying he wanted courts that didn't legislate from the bench. The Citizens United versus the FEC decision in 2010 was an astounding leap of legislation from what had been a case of being able to show the film Hillary: The Movie during election times. Somehow, the justice majority (5-4) decided to go a step further and just say it didn't matter who or with how much money political advertisements could spend on an election. Many are still dumbfounded on how this leap could have occurred.

Make no mistake, in the early days of the country, the very rich were big movers and shakers in bringing about our form of government. Even then they were extremely concerned that it could go back in the direction of a House of Lords, taking pains to make sure it wouldn't happen. They made laws to limit inheritance. In ensuing years, after seeing the development of large corporations, there were laws passed to limit monopolies.

The Citizens United decision gave Big Business the opening to influence elections by removing previous restraints on the amount they could spend and keep the donor list from being known. I'd like to emphasize "Big Business." Big Business by its very nature does not need any more assistance to influence anything. It's already BIG! I am in favor of giving small business better chances for success than the already large corporations. Small businesses need help. Deep pocketed businesses should not be allowed to influence elections. This is exactly opposite of what the original framers of the constitution envisioned.

The Citizens United decision must be repealed by law. Free speech is meant for individuals, not corporations. We can't let Big Money purchase elections. It's time to starve Big Money out of buying our elections. Spending that money on manufacturing jobs would be a better use of their resources.

Political ads by PACs typically present a candidate's position without having to verify there is any truth to what they are saying, leaving an emotional impression about what someone would do in office. We need laws that only allow an advertisement claiming a candidate's position, must be vetted by that candidate or party. No one should be allowed to put words into someone else's mouth without that person's okay. That's not free speech; that's just free fiction. I am tired of third-party negative campaigning. Hopefully, you are, too.

BIG money financing political ads needs to end. Allowing PACs to collect money from anonymous donors is not personal freedom of speech. It allows those with the most money to have greater influence over politics. Laws must be passed so candidates can speak for themselves. Repealing the Citizens United decision is a must.

3. "A spoonful of sugar helps the medicine go down,
    in the most delightful way!" From Disney's original
    Mary Poppins movie.

We'll get back to the sugar later. National Healthcare, a concept whose time has come. The other top twenty-five industrialized nations have it. We spend more money on it per capita—by far—and not everyone is getting it! Our current longevity is trending downward. This picture can and must be fixed.

How to go about it? Medicare for all? That would be an incomplete start. How about getting the options that our fearless compatriots in Congress receive? Better. Paying for it is a sticky point. Getting efficient use of our dollars for it would help immensely. Let's begin with that. It's a complex story.

We spend at least 20 percent more of our money per person than any other country. National Healthcare will save that right out of the gate. Think not about what it will cost but how much we'll save, because we will save by ending the current method of paying for it. And, we are already paying for our healthcare one way or another. The noise against it fails to mention we're already paying for our nation's health bill, but we're not getting full value for our dollar.

The insurance industry will have to take a severe hit on this one. There is no way around it. The Affordable Care Act was pooh-poohed by the Republicans, of course, including saying there would be death squads to decide who would live or die. The insurance companies were already doing that. Before the ACA, my doctor prescribed a medicine for allergies which I took to my favorite pharmacy. There I was told the insurance company wouldn't cover it without my doctor informing them what I was receiving the medication for. Who's in charge here, the doctor or the insurance company? Insurance company 1, doctor 0.

In Washington state, where I live, Boeing's one hundred thousand (give or take) employees have some clout in that regard and are able to negotiate better deals due to the size of the population base for that insurance. Also, in Washington state, you can get a number of options through various insurers with your employer, ACA, or any number of other private options. The point being the average person's clout in a small insurance pool is very minimal.

Single payor. Why isn't the entire country the group that gets to negotiate the deals? In any individual state there are more than one hundred different insurance plans in each which spreads out any potential for getting a better deal with individual plans. Divide and conquer provides the victory campaign for the insurance companies.

That brings up the next point. Why should our healthcare be dependent on some CEO's bonus or stock dividend? This is where the Republicans start shouting "Socialism." They think, why the heck can't somebody make a buck off your going to the doctor? Personally, this is a "middleperson" we can surgically remove from the equation and instantly realize better use of our healthcare dollars. Our healthcare should not be subject to the whims of corporate executives, ever. The corporate boardroom should not make healthcare decisions.

Wait, I hear the conservatives crying, "Socialism! Communism!" I have words for them, too. Despite the "affordable" options being presented today, there are millions of Americans who currently can't afford healthcare. Let's cry, "Inhumane!" Their health problems are worsening when they could be getting better. People avoid the doctor due to out of pocket expenses. We all pay when they hit the Emergency Room.

For those of you who are new to your jobs and healthcare benefits I'd like to throw out this example of how it once worked. About thirty years ago my Achilles tendon snapped. I went into surgery two days later. A month or so later I saw the bill for that, but I had no out of pocket expenses! Nada! Who would get that these days? Once upon a time there were no copays and once upon a time wasn't so very long ago.

In the nearly thirty years I worked at a hospital, the coverage went from excellent to where it is today. The insurance companies still get their premiums, but now everyone gets copays and ponies up another three hundred to six thousand dollars until the insurance pays out. What happened?!

One thing that happened was the erosion of unions. I tried to get my group to join, but not everyone was on the same page. The great benefits we had to begin with were because the greater number of employees were covered by a union and some of their benefits trickled down, but not all of them. More on that later. Over the course of time, the health benefit went downhill.

So, single payor. Let's save billions by removing an unnecessary cost in the equation. As one group, let's negotiate the deals for health-care, prescriptions, dental, and eyecare. We shouldn't have to be cut up into small pieces with little voice. Let's have one BIG voice!

One part of the industry that needs to be addressed properly are the hospitals. We need to keep them in business. That is another tricky question. In the years I worked at the hospital, new rules would be rolled out while at the same time Medicare reimbursements would be rolled back. This has resulted in people getting squeezed out of going where they want because doctors and medical centers just started re-fusing to accept new Medicare patients.

Our hospitals need to be maintained because we need their ex-pertise. In times of disaster we need their beds and greater capabilities. We had any number of disaster training events involving regional centers and how they would work together to spread out responses to weather, pandemic, earthquake, or industrial disasters. Our collec-tive health is dependent on our centers of care being able to maintain operation. Any calculations for total healthcare costs must include keeping our hospitals healthy and robust.

How to pay for it? They whom would have their children and their children's children pay for their mistakes will say it will be too expen-sive and bring about wholesale socialism, and they don't want to pay for that. Except, we already pay for it, and we pay too much. Wikipedia tells me that in 2015 health expenditure in the US was about $3.2 trillion, nearly 18 percent of the gross domestic product (GDP). That figure can drop tremendously once we have taken profit out of your healthcare decisions. Even for the Child Haters, that will be money in their pockets.

Wikipedia also informs that in the 2018 budget, Medicare and Medicaid expenditures were $972 billion, in round numbers, so, the first trillion is about accounted for. Removing the insurance middle person brings the total figure down another 20 percent, which roughly amounts to $600 billion removed from the equation. Previously mentioned, as a country, we pay approximately 20 percent more per capita than the next country on the list. Actual savings once we are a single payor nation may be greater.

We still have a gap to close. Initially, transitioning to true National Healthcare will be complicated and take some time before it will settle into a routine. Such change can't occur overnight. Currently, large employers already pay into healthcare plans, they can continue this through the near future and maybe always, but there are other possible revenue sources.

Remember that spoonful of sugar? I can't thank Wikipedia enough for the conglomeration of interesting facts; the US leads the world in sugar consumption! Yes, another thing we excel at, apparently at the rate of 4.4 ounces a day. Whew! Who knew? In my favorite state of

Washington, vice taxes range highest in the nation. Taxing sugar to help offset health costs makes so much sense, perhaps that portion could be prioritized towards diabetes.

Eventually companies selling sugary products would reduce the amount of sugar and sugar substitutes to cut down on this tax incursion. That's a win-win. As the health of the nation improves with National Healthcare, the cost of healthcare will go down. In twenty years, our longevity may vault past those countries already blessed with National Healthcare.

I've also heard it said there are people who don't want a government handout to live with. It's not a handout. You pay for it. Everyone already pays for it. We pay for everything and always will, that is how it works. It's a benefit that living in the wealthiest country in the world should provide. The wealthiest will still have their opportunity to pay for their tucks and Botox separately. No one is going to stop them. In the meantime, we can have the rallying cry, "A Spoonful of Sugar!" to get this National Benefit which everyone should be able to enjoy. Go ahead, support National Healthcare, have a donut!

4. "12.3% of Americans live below the poverty line."
    (2017) Wikipedia, again, thanks

The minimum wage needs to be brought up to a semblance of a living wage. Currently at $7.25 per hour, this largesse brings in about $1,300.00 monthly, not enough for one person to live on. Australia is way ahead of us on this one, $19.49 per hour. Should we allow the Aussies to have that bragging right? No!

Fifteen dollars per hour is a good start. I know you conservatives will say the economy will crash, candies will be stolen from babies, and we'll be irrevocably plunged into economic oblivion. Don't worry, women will only get $13.60 per hour. Just kidding! That's another issue.

It's true that raising the minimum wage in this aggressive fashion will alter the cost of numerous essentials. Hamburgers could cost a quarter more. Restaurants would raise prices, and a lot of small businesses would have to evaluate their payroll. On the positive side, more people will be able to afford more things. Overall, the economy would grow as more things would be affordable to more people. Trickle up! Let's give it a try!

In 2016 there was a lot of talk about income inequality, even the child haters brought up this disturbing fact. They will never act on this, though, because they don't want to pay for anything. Some of them may even think a slave economy would be better. There are employers that like a pool of disenfranchised people out there that can only get low paying jobs. Job satisfaction? Not on your life.

In the hospital I worked, nurses could be paid fifty dollars or more per hour. I have no problem with that; nursing is just not for everyone. The cleaning crew, whom they relied on to get rooms ready for the next patient and of whom they would speak glowingly, ten dollars an hour? Ask anyone, is their job to clean the room essential to the care of patients? Yes! Any job that someone is to be paid for is essential, otherwise the job would not exist. If it's a job, it's essential!

Everyone deserves to be paid a living wage. A living wage makes a person feel better about what they're doing. Job satisfaction will always relate to being able to pay the bills. Income inequality can only be addressed by bringing up the lowest wages and indexing them with the economy. Everyone's job is needed, whether they're sweeping the hallway or performing heart surgery. Fifteen dollars per hour is a start.

Local economies differ and various jurisdictions have already instituted higher wages. It is a process to bring local economies into the living wage arena. It is worth it for everyone. There will be some inflation, but nothing that can't be overcome. In the '70s, the gas crisis hit. One day I paid a dollar and got about four gallons of gas! What days those were! Suddenly we were paying twice as much. It was overnight! Gas lines at the service station stretched around the block. We survived.

A living wage won't be as traumatic as that was. There will be adjustments to our attitudes on the cost of services we routinely use. Restaurants will cost more, but maybe we can also adopt the Aussie way of not needing to tip everyone for everything. That may be a hard habit to break, or maybe not! More people will be able to afford to go out. The restaurants will win! The naysayers will claim the economy will tank. It will adapt, it always has, it always will. Some of us remember when they said computers would take away jobs. That should make you laugh.

The economy will adapt. People will have more job satisfaction. I'm going to bring up Australia again. I had the great fortune to visit there in 2014, when their minimum wage was $16.80. At the time, the exchange was about $1.05 to our dollar. Wherever we went, whatever people we ran into doing their jobs, we encountered smiling faces. Tourism is a big industry there. People were happy doing their jobs. I think it's because they were receiving a living wage. Of course, they also had National Healthcare. Generally, people were very positive. Let's get positive here, too!

Most jobs are already paying more than the minimum, but based on my math, thirty-six million people in this country are living below the poverty line. How many more just barely above? We must raise the tide. The only way to accomplish it is setting a livable minimum wage. Trickle down policies have never helped 99 percenters, ever. Let's stop borrowing money for the people who already have it. Everyone deserves a living wage. Let's make life, liberty, and the pursuit of happiness attainable for all!

5. "When you come to the end of your rope, tie a knot and hang on." Franklin Delano Roosevelt

I bring him into this discussion because he started Social Security. It must be sustained, and people should have confidence in it providing income for them in their later years. Conservatives have hated it from the start and likely chose to keep borrowing from it just to make it fail. An evil plan hatched seventy years ago? Hmmm.

Those of us in the 99 percent group feel this is a program that should be maintained and fully funded. Though it was never intended that it would be a person's sole income in retirement, it provides a consistent monthly payout that people should be able to rely on. The child haters wish to privatize this so their benefactors can make a profit off the government. We can't let that happen.

The conservatives believe in only two things, reduce taxes, reduce government. I'm not sure how they get elected to run the thing which they seek to destroy. We had a revolution to throw off the yoke of a "noble" class. Let's not give it back to them. We have earned a right, through our own labors, to receive the benefit of a steady income to get us through our twilight years.

Privatization only leads to evermore reductions and a lack of social responsibility. There is no need to change the system to one where decisions are made at the whim of some disconnected CEO intent on increasing his stock options. We already get enough of that.

Social Security as a program is solvent. The problem has been that its funds have been utilized for other purposes. Untie those purposes from the program and the system can continue providing retired workers with a steady and inflation-proof income. It is essential people have this source to look forward to and ease their minds for when they get to their golden years.

Private pension plans have been disappearing like telephone land-lines. It's because corporations have been moving people into 401ks and taking out the expense of maintaining a pension plan. Pension plans also gave people a great sense of security about the future because of the fixed guaranteed income they would provide. Today's young workers aren't seeing pensions offered much in the current job market. That is another of the many roadblocks seen by young workers, keeping them from believing in the hope of life, liberty, and the pursuit of happiness.

We need Social Security. Maybe we can ensure its solvency if we tie Congress's pension plan to it. Yes, they get their own separate, greater, and unequal pension plan. What if they had to rely on Social Security? That would get them to pay proper attention to the program.

The thought of tying their pension plan in with Social Security brings a smile. What if all the previously retired senators and congrespeople had their pensions reverted to Social Security. Would that prompt some action by the current members? I say, "Yes!" Still smiling. It's time to return trust in the system and end the talk of it not being around for the current workers who are contributing to it and those who have already contributed and depend on it.

6. "Infrastructure is job one!" You can quote me
    for that

Everyone wants a good job. Taking care of our infrastructure is of paramount importance. There was lip service by He Who Would Be King regarding taking care of infrastructure while campaigning. Once in, though, he had to take care of his own, borrowing money from us to give to those who already have it. Afterward, he said paying for infrastructure would mean reducing things like Medicaid, Medicare, Social Security, and food stamps. These are, after all, the "Entitlements" which every conservative says is holding our country back. It seems to me the greatest benefactors of the tax legislation enacted favored those who consider themselves entitled.

Getting back to the job at hand, we need our roads, bridges, water supplies, utilities, and our waste properly attended to. Private enterprise will not take care of these issues, unless you would like to pay a toll for road service every time you go to the grocer. The backlog of essential maintenance and replacement of these necessary items is growing. Putting it off puts us in greater danger and that costs more in the long run.

These things need to be paid for. We can take back the money we gave to the 1 percent to pay for these things we need. How many more bridges will fall, water systems fail, or power outages occur, leaving us at the mercy of the weather, before we act? There are so many jobs that need to be done there could probably be no joblessness. All jobs create more jobs, it's a known economic fact.

After the Bush Recession and Obama came into office, the Republicans choked off public funds, resulting in large layoffs throughout the government. The math is that for every two government jobs, one gets created in the private sector in support. The Grinches of anti-government sat back in glee as they watched the ever-growing unemployment lines getting attributed to Obama. They knew fewer government jobs would mean layoffs in private industry. You can be sure it saddened them when the economy began to recover within a year, starting off another round of expansion that continued throughout the Obama administration. The resiliency of America once again triumphed!

The Grinches were not happy. How could their plan backfire so miserably? We do need infrastructure jobs, and it shouldn't be put off any longer. Let's pony up the funds and put US back to work, with good wages. No one wants to read more stories about falling bridges or municipal water systems going bad. Despite what the unemployment figures show, some who lost jobs and homes during the recession never fully recovered. They either never got another well-paid job or lost benefits that never got replaced, including their homes.

Bottom line on any job creation is that you and I pay for these jobs, through government or private enterprise. How we spend our money determines how industries come and go. Our wallets are voting machines on which industries live or die. Because so many people are finding it easier to shop online, brick and mortar stores are disappearing. It is personally distressing for me because I like to know more about what I'm getting and where it's made, for instance.

I like to buy things made in the USA. I'm old enough to see how dramatically that changed in the last twenty years. It not only is difficult to find; there is the sticker shock if you are lucky enough to find it. Typically, I find the product made here will last far longer than the cheap product overseas, but the temptation to save money for what may appear to be an adequate replacement is great. Often what you "saved" money on turns out to be a rental, not a purchase. You get to buy a shiny new one, again, a year or less later.

We have the power to bring manufacturing back to the US, but it will take some willpower at the store—or shopping site. You may even find it difficult to locate the country of origin. Then it's time to be more wary. The copycat industry makes products which you believe are from your manufacturer of choice, but it's a knockoff from somewhere offshore, another rental. It becomes harder and harder to find good products for purchase as opposed to paying good money for a rental. Getting value for your dollar is now about evaluating quality over quantity.

Paying attention to where a product is made, though not everyone's cup of tea, does pay dividends. I've saved a lot of dough just shedding one country off my purchase list. Make a game of it for your amusement. In the long run, you'll be ahead. Good luck! Vote for quality with your wallet!

Nothing is more American than building roads, constructing new homes, office buildings, and the general maintenance of infrastructure. Infrastructure makes cities and civilization possible. (Please believe civilization is possible in our time!) Striving for the betterment of society is what has always kept us at the forefront of innovation and technological advancement. Let's step forward, wallets in hand, or better yet, wallets of the 1 percent in hand, and get our infrastructure on!

7. "If you think education is expensive, try ignorance."
    Attributed to Ann Landers and Derek Bok, while
    president of Harvard

Education must be included in the top things for Congress to address. Education leads to everything. Innovation, a better life, people who can do the math to balance a budget. It really is a necessary part of the equation to making the country stronger and smarter. Any discussion of education must start at the beginning.

The first five years of a child's life is when their brains grow the most. Their future grasp of education is dependent on how much they learn in their critical first years. This has been clearly established. So, first things first, we need to ensure the ability of all children to get access to learning at the earliest possible stages. Daycare must include introducing children to letters, numbers, and reading. Ideally, daycare should be universally available or affordable for all.

Also, a good breakfast, lunch, and dinner goes a long way towards making sense out of this life. Healthy foods should be available to all children. Children should not have to pay for the errors of adults. Yes, poor people have babies. Those babies need good nutrition. Helping to get the neediest children good food options should be a priority. Raising the tide means ending the cycle of inherited poverty.

The intelligence level a child gets to in their first years of life determines their future abilities. This is where education begins. K-12 is essential, but it all starts earlier than that. It's good we make education mandatory for our children in all states. We just need to start earlier.

Of course, I don't want to take away anyone's childhood. Fun is fun, and kids need to learn how to have fun, too. Some childhoods seem endless, even with the well-to-do, just look at Donald the First. A few kids just never grow up. Social skills are also part of a well-rounded upbringing.

Establishing a firm grasp of mathematics brings benefits that last a lifetime. Some might say they would never use algebra in their adult lives. It's the critical thinking processes it creates which help in making good decisions. Like balancing a budget.

Reading and writing give skills which never go out of style. The three Rs go a long way in any person's life. The earlier the better. Free primary education is the single best thing government provides.

In high school though, individuals begin to discover interests outside of the basics. Unfortunately, funding for this has dried up as time as gone by. Auto mechanics has been taken out of schools. Despite the tech wave kids ride these days, gear heads are still out there.

Wood shop can start people on a career in carpentry. It is an art that should never be lost. The electrical trades and construction can be introduced. Maritime careers, cuisine, fashion and design interest a variety of students. Their interest in these areas and curiosity should be rewarded.

STEM courses, a personal favorite, should always be stressed. Innovation drives the world's economy, and STEM is essential for the country to remain a leader in industry. Though it's not for everyone, all kids deserve the educational opportunities to advance them into adulthood.

Then there's college. A college education should be attainable for all. Student loans as a percentage of personal debt has risen to an all-time high. It is an anchor preventing young adults from prospering in today's world. This one thing has brought disillusionment to countless folk of our emerging generations.

Income inequality and rising housing costs have driven the new generation into despair. They feel the American Dream is out of reach for them. They blame their parent's generation for leaving them in this predicament. Of course, I say it was my parent's generation that did this…kidding aside, blame here isn't the issue. Solutions should be the topic.

Education is the one thing that will continue to move us forward. Accessibility needs prioritizing for all levels. Perhaps the tech companies could provide funding for our universities to expand STEM classes instead of begging for more H1-B visas. Industry could provide dollars for college training. Education is not an option; it is a necessity. Let's properly fund it.

8. "Let me sum up," Inigo Montoya from
The Princess Bride

The basic talking points:

1.   Repeal the Citizens United decision

2.   National Healthcare

3.   Living Wage Minimum $15

4.   Social Security stabilization

5.   Infrastructure = Jobs

6.   Education

On 1, we can't allow big money to continue to influence elections unchecked.

On 2, it's just time we got this done; the current system has no merit.

On 3, it's trickle up time! Raise the tide, and the tide will rise for all.

On 4, the nation needs this sigh of relief.

On 5, jobs, infrastructure, a clear win-win.

On 6, education is the foundation for all.

As our candidates go through their campaigns, the shouting from conservatives will be typical. Taxes will go up! Socialism! That's all they've got. Coming up with policy which benefits the greater population isn't an option. It goes against their religious belief which is limited to "No Taxes and No Government." The only go-to policy they insist on repeating is borrowing money to give to billionaires. Even though it's been proven time and again to raise the deficit without any economic benefit.

They won't discuss policies of any merit, because for them it's "inconceivable." You'll hear, "government needs to be run more like a business." Do you starve business of its resources? No, but that is the result of their singular policy. How about running a business with deficits year in and year out? Not a way to run any enterprise. Bad math is the hallmark of the modern Conservative.

Since discussing policy is beyond their typical focus, the Child Haters like to throw out this question instead of responding to questions, "Capitalist or Socialist?" The new favorite question in retort could be, "Socialist for the Rich or Democracy?" Our current regime tends towards the former. This has opened many eyes to the alarming fact that supporting Rich Socialism includes racism, fascism, and anarchy.

Which is why we need to get the deep pockets out of influencing elections. The PAC ads use scare tactics and put words into the mouths of candidates. Only candidates should be allowed to state what their beliefs and motivations are.

It's also time we joined the first world countries which have National Healthcare. Unbelievably, I just read a story where a man in his seventies called 911 in Ferndale, Washington, to inform them he was killing his wife and himself because of medical bills! This shouldn't happen in the wealthiest country. It also shows that Medicare for all doesn't go far enough. Let's get National Health right. Make it cover everyone, including the lawmakers, so they'll be sure to make it work for all.

There is no quicker solution for income inequality than raising the minimum wage to a living wage. If it's a job someone needs to be paid to do, then it is a job that needs to be rewarded with a living wage. Just as in a hospital where the person bringing food to the patient, cleaning, nursing, or performing surgery are all essential; any job that needs to be done deserves to be paid out in living wages.

On Social Security, people need to have confidence there will be this guaranteed amount they can look forward to getting in their later years. It wasn't intended to be the only source for them, though for some, it is one thing that they can hang rely on. Not everyone is a CPA who can be counted on to make great decisions for their future. Some may be misled, intentionally or not, by those who are qualified advisors. Social Security is the cushion people should be able to depend on.

Taking care of infrastructure will bring good jobs. There has been a long period of deferred maintenance in this regard. Getting back up to speed will bring jobs all over the country. Road, water and utility systems need addressing. In Seattle, there are one-hundred-year-old water pipes made of tree trunks. What's your city using? There are no credible arguments for letting necessary systems fall apart.

Our candidates will have to be strong to stick to these guns under the usual tactics thrown by the Rich Socialists. There may even be some name calling along the way. The Child Haters use emotional words all the time. They'll bring up their opponents will raise taxes. They won't tell you that, as a nation, we pay the LEAST taxes of the industrialized world. There is no time like the present, in a growing economy, as the richest country on the planet, to cover our bills and pay down the collective debt.

For some, the allure of paying less appeals to our basic instinct to save a buck. I've found that if you spend your money right the first time, you save in the long run. For instance, why build a stadium to use for only twenty years? Fenway Park and Wrigley Field have been in use for over a hundred years! It doesn't make sense just to do things the cheapest way possible. Let's admit we're in it for the long haul and build it to last. People are still going to the Coliseum in Rome, nearly two thousand years later!

9. "What can we do as individuals?" - My question…
    the list goes on

Democracy is a participation activity. Vote! Voting is the single most important right to exercise. There can be no more, "Oh, I'm not very political." The last general election showed us neglecting to vote can be mind-numbingly devastating. His Lordship, Donald the First, won without the benefit of a majority. Personally, I am tired of seeing my vote count for less than someone else's vote. It's not the first time this century this occurred.

Voting has been compromised in several states. Gerrymandering is well out of control in Georgia, North Carolina, and Wisconsin. These three states have also been on the forefront of indiscriminately removing voters from eligibility lists, in the name of voter fraud. Removing voters from the eligibility list is voter fraud. It's the sort of thing Fascists do, taking away the right to vote.

Don't let your right be taken away! It is the greatest right ever given by any government. We had a revolution to secure that right. Many people died to give us that right. It is that right which separated us from the "nobility" of British rule. There are millionaires and billionaires out there who would very much like to use their wealth to keep us 99 percenters from voting against them. Not all of them, of course, but their wealth has put them in a position to abuse the power the wealth has given them.

We don't need to return to the system we threw off over two hundred years ago. I was recently surprised to read the latest Prime Minister of England was only voted in by a relatively small cadre of one hundred thousand casting their privileged votes. This, in a country of over sixty million? Something is wrong with that picture!

Vote every time. Love to vote. It is a luxury afforded to us by people who thought there was a better way to govern. People died to give us this privilege. You don't have to be in love with who you vote for. Yes, it seems it's just the lesser of two evils on occasion, but vote! The more you vote, the more likely better people will run. We should be garnering 85 percent or more of those eligible every primary and general election.

Low voting rates lets a minority control the elections. Typically, the hate government, don't tax group, votes every time. They're 30 – 35 percent of the population. At the meager 50 percent voter turnout rate, that gives them the majority of the votes in many elections. So, you see, there is hope to bring change through the ballot box. Putting people in office that believe government serves a purpose should be our goal. Allowing those who would destroy that which we currently have a say in, goes against us. Please vote.

Get your friends to vote! Instead of taking people's votes away from them, government should give tax breaks for those that do vote in the primaries and general elections. Incentives to increase participation could get us above that 85 percent threshold.

If the Fascists were serious about voter fraud, they would ensure there is a paper trail for all elections. I like what the state of Washington has done. Vote by mail. Everyone gets a ballot delivered to their home, and now, postage is included! No more lines at the local school or designated polling station. Two weeks, or more, to fill out your ballot, in the comfort of your own home. Guaranteed to count. We also have designated drop-off sites if you'd rather not trust the postal service with your precious vote.

Every state needs to have a proper paper trail for all elections. Organize in your state to put that on the ballot. Mail-in ballots for all is a great way to encourage voter turnout. Another handy way to get people on the rolls is the Motor Voter system we have also put in place in Washington. If you get a driver's license, you get registered to vote. Use your power to poll; it doesn't take much time, but the reward is helping to make a difference. Democracy is a participation activity. Be active, all you need do is vote.

10. "…You can fool some of the people all of the
     time…" Abe Lincoln

Were Abe to run for office today, many in his party would be shouting
him down. Making it to the general election would be out of reach for
him. The Tea Party has wrested control with anti-government, anti-tax
single-mindedness that would surely exclude Abe from the mix for
modern Republicans.

Fomenting the Deep State paranoia and representing government
as bad is keeping the birther and conspiracy theorists full of fodder to
fuel this fantasy. Government may not always be the most efficient, but
it should have the interest of the average person. Except for maybe the
picture takers at the Department of Licensing. There may be some conspiracy there.

Fake news is a recurring topic. Donald the First excels at making
up his own stories and facts. The mainstream media is portrayed as
slanted and unreliable. The legitimate newspapers and television programs are attacked. If you look up something on the internet, you're
likely to find "facts" which contradict each other. However, the mainstream media has professionals who go out of their way to research
news and back up what they print or say. They take pride in accuracy
and research.

Fox News has pointed out they are an entertainment channel. When you watch it, though, it represents itself as a news organization when it rather operates as an opinion center. Some people don't choose to dig too deeply for underlying facts. They would rather bolster their opinions with others who reinforce those opinions. Who needs concrete evidence when you can just find someone who will agree with you?

Another thing we get to hear from the Child Haters is how successful the tax cut package has been. It's like watching a movie; don't let the muddled facts keep you from sitting back and enjoying the show. Bad math is epidemic in the supply-side camp. Supply-side economics have only ever raised the deficit and left more bills unpaid. The only "upside" is that people with great wealth get to have even more money, which we borrowed to give to them. The frustration level over this horrifically bad policy is overwhelming.

Forgive me as I bring up again that we had a revolution over two hundred years ago to throw off the shackles of these "noble" birthers. Here we are today, enabling them to hang on to what they already have. This privileged class gets to use our money to spend on PACs so they can keep more of it. It's a spiral that can only be ended by voting out the modern blue bloods and overturning the Citizens United decision through legislation.

Let's take out the bad math group and vote in fiscally responsible people who can balance a budget. In 2018 we paid $325 billion on interest alone and borrowed more than that to cover the rest of the bills. This must stop. There is no logical explanation for driving the collective debt any higher when the economy thrives. We can and should cover the cost of running the country.

Yes, "less government" and "less taxes" shouters are religious on this issue, and how it all makes perfect economic sense, if only you would believe. In the religion I was raised in, we were informed we must pay for our sins. I'm not saying funding the government is a sin, because funding the government is for the collective good, the betterment of society, and maintaining a semblance of civilization. Let's just pay our bills and pay down the debt. It will create a better sense of well-being in the nation.

Foisting today's debts onto future generations is total fiscal irresponsibility. It simply can't be justified with logical, cogent argument. The Child Haters disagree, of course. For them, it is the ultimate achievement of Capitalism. What it is, is the ultimate achievement of a failure to do math. Clearly, the GOP are mathematically challenged. We need to propose that no elected representative should be allowed the responsibility of government service without passing a high school math test with an emphasis on algebra.

Our representative's education should not be left behind!

11. "United We Stand, Divided, We Fall!" Abe, again

Those of us old enough to remember readily finding goods Made in America also might remember the heady days before medical copays began. Slowly, inexorably, medical costs were put on the worker, relieving large employers of one of the biggest benefit costs. All the benefits we've ever gotten as workers can be attributed to Unions.

Unions brought us the eight-hour day, the forty-hour week, weekends, holidays, sick leave, vacation pay, pensions, medical, vision, and dental plans. Some would portray unions as a big monster that takes money out of your paycheck. Organized labor isn't a big monster. It's you and your coworkers joining together to negotiate a better working situation.

Many of those who see unions as another institution to distrust are probably the same ones who distrust government. In our government and every union, everyone gets a vote. Participation is an individual's responsibility, but as we know, our vote may not always be on the winning side. Being in a union means you have a group that will back you up and work towards more favorable workplace outcomes.

Union membership started to erode in the '80s with a concerted effort by large corporations and the New Feudal Lords. They would sell off portions of the company, and the "new" one would get to hire or fire you after letting you apply for your job back. The "new" company wouldn't already have a union, and so union busting became a tactic of business, by divesting portions of their business.

It was in the '80s that health insurance plans began to introduce the copay. It's been downhill for the average worker ever since. Off-shoring was another tactic to reduce union jobs. Once it was common to see "Proudly Made in the USA" followed by a Union label. People held their heads higher because they were a part of something greater than just the individual. Unions helped to institute pride in the workplace.

It has all been eroded by the concerted efforts of the Barons of Businesses. This is the same group that instills a distrust in government. Divide and conquer. That has worked for corporate America. Time to reverse course.

Becoming part of a Union shouldn't be scary or repulsive. It's joining into a group with the common goal of better wages and benefits. Better job security. Better conditions to work under and a grievance process with a representative to help you with your case!

How this is presented as bad, is hard to conceive. Groups always get listened to more than any individual. A "Right to Work" state is just a right to waive your right to be organized and get better benefits and pay. The small group of people I worked with included some who didn't want to pay union dues. Our pensions were capped while the represented employees still had theirs grow.

Think about it. Would you rather go into Human Resources by yourself to state your cause? Or would you rather present to Human

Resources as a group willing to stand together for everyone's benefit? Go on! Join or start a Union today! In the long run, you'll be better off for it. United We Do Stand!

12. "…You can't fool all the people all of the time."
    Abe, again

People's feelings can be manipulated. It happens on the internet "all the time." Emotional appeals at distrusting the government. Encouraging folks to vote in people who don't believe in government. Turns out that is just anarchy to benefit the wealthy. There are a variety of names for governments run by moneyed interests.

Money will always have an influence. Any government, dictatorship, monarchy, or communist plot will be influenced by money. In a democracy, voting can limit the control money has over our lives. It's okay to say that concentrating money into fewer and fewer hands is bad for the general welfare. By saying so, doesn't make one a Communist.

Concentrating money into fewer and fewer hands is Entitlement for the 1 percent. We are not the 1 percent. Let's try something new. Let's VOTE for something different. Trickle down has miserably funneled up. Time to turn the tide, Trickle Up! Raising the tide really will float more boats. Let's take the concept to new heights.

My hopes and dreams hinge on people taking a greater interest in making this government of ours better. All it takes is a vote. Get out there and do it. At twice a year, this simple act empowers us to be in charge. You won't always win but participating is a win. Get your friends, family and coworkers to vote.

The Lords of the Boardroom need to be reined in from buying elections. Letting them scare you into believing some candidate will take away your job or your various pursuits to happiness will only ensure they keep a bigger piece of the pie. Once again, we must throw off the shackles of the Entitled Rich.

If We the People exercise the right to vote, we can take charge of decision making. Having a proper paper trail for our vote keeps it honest and fair. Big Money should not be allowed to influence elections. If everyone votes, then we'll get what we deserve. Hmmm…might have to restate that.

Anyway, let's get away from the Citizens United decision by electing people who will legislate it out of existence. How corporations could be considered to have rights as individuals goes against all we had the American Revolution for. Let's not be fooled again.

13. "An investment in knowledge pays the best
     interest." Ben Franklin

Paying for college currently ranks high on the worry scale for those seeking higher education. In the state of Washington, during much of this century, tuition kept increasing well over inflation. "Starve the government" state representatives were happy enough with this. They heard the college educated vote against them at greater rates.

It's hard enough to keep track of my own state so I don't know what your state has been doing. Probably raising tuition. Here's a not so funny consequence, international students are getting into our universities at increasing rates, as much as 20 percent of enrolled. The other consequence of that is, it pushes our local folk out of classroom space.

International students are getting in because they're paying in at higher tuition rates. That's helping to offset the cost of running our colleges. Except it means fewer of our own get accepted. So, just to pay the bills, colleges are accepting greater numbers of foreign students. This is not the way to keep America ahead in innovation.

Employers are begging for more graduates in well-paying jobs. Universities are now trying to expand those sought-after programs. In the meantime, we need to find a way to pay for college education. Perhaps the industries which benefit the most from an educated work force can pony up. We need to come up with a way to end the cycle of debt for education.

Investing in education will always pay dividends. Benjamin Franklin would agree.

14. "The only thing we have to fear is fear itself."
Franklin Delano Roosevelt

If you believe in supply-side economics, what you've read so far in this book would probably instill more than fear. Outright panic. Words such as these will pour out of you, "Socialism!", "Communist Conspiracy!", "More Taxes!" If you believe in supply-side economics, even after having had paid attention for the last forty years, perhaps you also believe in the Tooth Fairy.

Supply-side economics have led to increasing deficits and the concentration of money into fewer and fewer hands. It's in the public record. If you believe in supply-side, it's really a Religion to you. As a devout believer, no amount of evidence against it will ever be enough for you. I'm impressed, though, that you've read this far.

As I'm willing to confess there will be an increase of taxes to pay for the things which civilization requires, I'm sure good old American Ingenuity and Capitalism will be able to provide all we need. Trickle Up will be a process and an adjustment but despite the Labels sure to be given to it by the Child Haters, the time is now to let us 99 percenters Raise the Tide.

Labels are the comfort food for the Righteous Right. Willingly increasing public debt for the benefit of few gives them a perfect right to be called Child Haters. Why do they choose to burden our offspring?

They just don't want to pay for anything. It is their Religion, first commandment. The only other commandment is No Government, essentially anarchy for the Large Corporate Sponsors.

Demonstrating fiscal irresponsibility time after time can't possibly be justified. It hasn't worked. Currently, we pay over three hundred billion dollars just to service the debt. Encouraging deficits which have stretched from four hundred billion dollars to nearly a trillion is no way to run a country—or a business. Because these Child Haters have said government should be run like a business, then let's pay our bills instead of dumping them on future generations.

Strong countries have strong governments. Working toward a Third World Debt situation will not make us strong. It will lead us to the same problems facing Greece. The concentration of money there is phenomenal. Let's turn the tide while the time is ripe. Raise the Tide! Trickle Up, it's the funnel thing to do.

15. The Equal Rights Amendment (I thank Alison
    Thoet of PBS with facts for this section)

With luck, this has already been ratified as you read this. Originally pro-
posed in 1972, thirty-eight states are required to ratify this and put it
into the Constitution. Thirty-eight have a now done so; what's the
holdup? We, as the original framers intended, consider the Constitution
to be a living document. Something to be improved upon as time goes
by. Others might say, "Chisel it in stone and let it be!"

The Declaration of Independence says, "We hold these truths to
be self-evident: that all men are created equal…". Eventually, slaves
were considered to be men! Another barbaric barrier crossed! Then,
just fifty-seven years later, women got the right to vote! Everyone was
included! Yay!

Unfortunately, as people of color and women know, equality is still
elusive. Roughly half the population, women, have yet to receive their
full half of the deal. Wages for women run significantly behind men. So
here we are, a hundred years from women's suffrage, and there is still
plenty of work to be done.

Any one of these twelve states could help right this inequity:

Alabama	Mississippi
Arizona	Missouri
Arkansas	North Carolina

Florida	Oklahoma
Georgia	South Carolina
Louisiana	Utah

What's the holdup? What has it been in these states that ensuring equal protections for half the population seems to be problematic? Looking around, it's easy to see that in the boardrooms, legislatures, and the vast array of business structure that equal representation is considerably lacking. Even given this boost of ratification, it will still take time before we see the benefit spread around properly.

Equality has been making slow progress in the last couple of decades, but we haven't seen the end of the barbarism of our ancestors, yet. Women are just as capable as men. Like men, their strengths and weaknesses vary. Everyone needs to be treated individually. Our strengths and weaknesses make it necessary that we work together, as equals.

Equality for race, religion, LGBTQ+, etc. may have been legislated to some degree in the various states, but there still needs to be work done on this Living Document, the Constitution. It can be accomplished. Changing people's minds and ingrained prejudices is another process.

Differences between people need to be put aside. The simple fact of the matter is we've got to work together. None of us is an island; making it through our day depends on thousands of other folks doing their jobs so we can have a home to go to, keep warm, and eat. We are codependents in civilization. Marginalizing people for their differences will never accomplish anything.

Yes, we have differences. Vive la difference!

16. "Tell me, and I forget. Teach me, and I remember. Involve me, and I learn." Ben Franklin

Education is central to everything. As previously stated, it should start as early as possible to create the greatest outcome. Education shouldn't stop once we've reached adulthood, however. It should especially be provided for adults whose jobs are being displaced by technology.

The Bush Recession left a mark that hasn't been properly addressed. So many people lost well-paying jobs that never got replaced. Sure, the numbers tell us that unemployment is historically low. Some folks never got another job or lost their home. Others are working at inadequately paying jobs because that is what they could find and benefits were lost.

Coal workers, whether they may want to admit it or not, are in an industry which is becoming extinct. The reasons are many, but the bottom line is these willing workers need to be retrained for modern jobs. Clean energy jobs should be encouraged to locate in the states where these good workers live. Transition isn't always easy for anyone who has lost a job. Providing a way for them to transition can make it better.

Other industries have provided career change education to their employees. Perhaps the coal industry can do the same. The truth is that coal is becoming economically less attractive. Some would say it's been regulated out of business. That's because sound health and environment are causes worth paying for.

Certainly, anyone who works with coal will have a lower life expectancy and experience health consequences. Those living near coal production get the same consequences. Cancer rates are higher due to coal production for those who live near mines or breathe the air from the power plants.

Consequences need to be considered for any industry. Doing something the cheapest way possible doesn't pencil out if all aspects of an industry are accounted for. Those who would condemn government regulations don't feel your health or environment are important. The regulations are there to protect us. They also create jobs.

Yes, regulation creates jobs. That's why it costs more to follow them. Some people may not like the jobs regulation creates, but those costs do directly go to making jobs. Industrialists tend towards just wanting to make things as cheaply as possible. Their p-patch isn't downstream from the strip mine. All they see is the line item on the balance sheet.

Coal can be produced in a clean manner. It just costs more to do so. That makes more jobs! It also makes it pencil out to just move to cleaner energy sources. Clean energy won't take away jobs; it is creating more jobs. Let's encourage those jobs to go to the coal states. It will lessen their health risks at the same time. Another win-win!

17. *Baby Steps*, a book by Dr. Marvin in the movie
     What About Bob?

Okay, I admit, filling out tax forms year in and year out is a source of stress and unwanted research. In my favorite state of Washington, they never have had us do income taxes. We pay as we go by having high sales and property taxes. Everyone knows this regressive system unduly burdens the less fortunate. However, we don't have to fill out extra forms every year to pay our state taxes. This is a source of joy in my house as I get to handle "doing the taxes" every year, and it's one less source of extra paperwork. Still, it is regressive.

What I like about the pay-as-you-go lifestyle is the lack of stress and forms designed by what can be imagined as beasts in dark chambers under the bowels of the earth. There may be a way to accomplish paying the taxman with less pain attached. Like "Baby Steps," I call it small bites. Here's my fun story to illustrate the principal:

At the young age of nineteen, I had the great fortune to spend some time in the Aloha State. Much of that time I was on the beaches, and at one beach, a pizza-eating contest was sponsored by a local hangout. Seven lucky people got to participate in it. The motley crew assembled consisted of a classically large Hawaiian man, another man who represented the skinny hippie crowd, another large man, a slender woman, a guy who looked Australian, and a couple of classic surfer dudes. The contest was to eat and swallow one piece of pizza first, the winner getting a large pizza as a reward.

It could have been a great opportunity to lay wagers based on girth or whatever sways the inner gambler. I watched as each of the contestants worked their way through their pieces. The skinny hippie savored every bite, not interested in victory. The others mostly tried to stuff their piece down their throats in a classic display of bad eating habits. The woman, however, took it one small bite at a time, swallowing with grace all the while until finishing her piece first. The others were mostly still choking. Free pizza to the small bite theorist! How about that!

Small bites are the easiest to take. We might not be able to small bite our way completely through the National Budget, but it is an approach that could make certain line items easier to swallow. More on the small bite theory applications as we progress. I stress progress.

18. "Plastics." Quote from Mr. Maguire to Benjamin in
    The Graduate

So true it was! Plastics are everywhere! That's the problem. They are everywhere in almost everything. My first paper shredder was well constructed, and I took it apart to fix it (it's what I do). Throughout the construction of the shredding mechanism there were solid metal parts all over. The one cog in there made of plastic had a tooth broken off. Part unavailable, new shredder.

Plastic can pay for more excellent jobs, like clearing the oceans of the swirling masses of plastic. There are fishing boats out there begging for work in an ever-dwindling industry. Let's send them out to net plastic. It's a natural fit. This will create more well-paid jobs and put some idle boats back to work. It will take quite a while to fish out that supply.

Small bites on the cost of plastic bags for instance. What if five cents for every box of twenty-five bags went for funding the cleanup of the oceans? That would produce jobs and help the idle fishing boats out there. The plastic manufacturers might cry they're being picked on. The Supply Siders would say it'll doom the plastic bag industry. Mostly, we would hardly notice.

Not all industries end up paying all the costs of their industry. We do, one way or the other. It's just putting the cost on the products. Other plastics manufacturers can have a similar, and equally unnoticeable to us, levy on their products. They already have accountants employed to handle the paperwork. Certainly, they will grumble about having to pay this tax. It won't break them. We'll be the ones to pony up, pennies at a time.

Good jobs good for the welfare of the oceans should be a priority for us. Even if you don't eat fish, the health of the oceans will always affect the health of us and the rest of the planet. Let's work towards cleaning up plastic waste, creating good jobs along the way, a few cents at a time. Small bites are easiest to swallow.

19. "You can't see the forest for the trees."
    Popular idiom

There's another way to pay for jobs and help the planet. The Trillion

Tree Initiative. This could have been my idea, but a study co-authored

by Thomas Crowther of the Swiss Federal Institute of Technology has

put forward this very plan. Let's pay for it with a five-cent-a-gallon gas

tax. It would pay for a lot of trees.

There have been stories about making machines that would chew

up the carbon in the air and oceans. We don't need technology for that,

just plant trees.

We humans need understand the simple truth that we've been

cutting down trees for thousands of years, maybe millions. This has

allowed desertification of countless areas across the planet. The Amer-

ican Southwest, Saharan and Sub-Saharan Africa, the Mideast, Australia,

South America, and in Asia. We've done this to the planet, slowly turn-

ing areas into desert.

The quickest and simplest way to turn this around is planting trees

back into the environment. Africa would be a great place to start, but

all continents need it. Shrink the Sahara by planting trees. Start in the

mountains. Bring in water from the secondary treatment plants to get

them started and flourishing. Once you've gotten a large enough swath of trees planted, that will lead to weather changes making it all self-sustaining. It might take fifty years, but it's worth it for the planet's sake.

It would help if people cutting trees for basic fuel needs were given another fuel source. This can be done, and there are some very efficient stoves and ovens out there that can serve this population. More cost, more jobs! Pay for consequences by tacking a few cents onto the cost of a gallon of gas. That is a small bite.

A trillion trees. Fifty years. We can do this. One tree at a time. For a mere five cents a gallon, we can make this a worldwide effort. Slow and steady can help win this race. Everyone benefits, and more jobs get created. The trees getting cut down would have to be subtracted from the total, but it would all be worth it. I can't wait for the count up to begin!

20.   The Cycle of Poverty can end. Believe it can be
       made so.

The history of serfdom is the history of poverty. The Lords controlled the land and wealth. The serfs got to work the land and keep pennies on the pound for their labors. Though our forebears eliminated nobles from the equation by evicting the British Lords, serfdom still exists in the form of today's minimum wage.

Unchanged now for over ten years, it was inadequate even then. According to federalsafetynet.com, individual poverty is considered to be living on $34 per day which works out to $12,410 per year. The current minimum wage, $7.25/hour comes out to $14,500 per year. For ninety-nine percent of us, that would not be considered living.

Certain industries like to have a supply of cheap labor to make their ends meet. The inadequate minimum wage doesn't instill a sense of pride in workmanship. How dedicated of an employee would you expect? If a job is needed, then it should be paid at livable levels. Will this raise the cost of a given widget? Yes. Most people would rather spend good money on a well-produced product than one where no pride can be derived from its making.

New York and Seattle have already instituted fifteen-plus-dollar minimum wages. Before that there were the typical outcries about how raising the minimum would destroy the local economies. The destruction never took place. Just as when gas—and energy—prices doubled, the economy adjusted.

Home ownership is still out of reach of those in these and other high-priced local economies. Bringing the minimum to fifteen dollars is just the start to Raising the Tide for all. Yes, the cost of a given widget will go higher, but not unaffordable. Your favorite burger might go up twenty-five cents. More people will be able to buy those burgers. The economies of scale, quantity sales driving prices lower, might make the increase moot.

Pride in the workplace makes a better product. Income inequality gets somewhat balanced. More people could afford Made-In-America products! I miss the days, just twenty years ago, when "Proudly made in the USA," accompanied by a union trademark, was far more commonplace.

Look at product labels and support American made products if you can find them. It may be harder to find, but it will be worth the added expense. Certainly, it will last longer. Let's make the products better by paying better wages. Pride of Workmanship and Pride of Ownership go hand in hand.

I know how hard it is at the department store, comparing prices. Deciding which to buy and not wanting to part with any more money than absolutely necessary. Start thinking about what may be a Better Purchase or Just a Rental. That extra money isn't an arm or a leg you're removing. It's an investment.

Let's Raise the Tide, investing in our fellow Americans! Upping the minimum wage is the first step toward income equality. WE deserve it! At nearly twenty dollars per hour, the Australians shouldn't be the only ones happy with their jobs.

21. "…the only way to lower the record-high federal deficit would be to cut Entitlement programs like Medicare, Medicaid and Social Security." Mitch McConnell, Oct '18

Faced with increasing deficits after enacting the Entitlements for the Rich and Powerful tax cut, the Child Haters want the less fortunate and retirees to help balance the budget. Some of the people who have been fooled all of the time voting for the fiscally irresponsible, need to see the light of how they have been led down a spiraling path of deficit spending that they and their offspring will pay for.

First Reagan, then W, now Donald the First, have borrowed money to give the Privileged a bigger cut of the pie. Each time it was with promises it would stimulate the economy and pay for itself. Each time it has resulted in escalating deficits. The record speaks for itself. It will never work. Why, in times of a healthy economy, shouldn't we just pay our bills? Pay down the debt while we're at it.

These Child Haters have been successful at concentrating the nation's wealth into fewer and fewer hands. That's in the record. It can't be hidden. The Top Three of Forbes 400 Wealthiest have approximately $350 billion, the bottom 140 million Americans have approximately $250 billion. (from Inequality.org) I did the math on that. It comes out to about $1,786.00 each. Yikes!

Now is the time to turn the tide. Social Security doesn't need reduction. Perhaps we can offset Social Security costs by having Congress's generous pension plan replaced by Social Security and their retirement incomes can go to keeping the system afloat. Just throwing out ideas here. It might make legislators pay a little more attention.

Medicaid, Medicare, and Social Security aren't "entitlements" to be discarded. They are systems we've paid into and earned. Anyone who refers to these programs we've paid into as "entitlements" are the ones who should be cut out of making decisions with our money.

Having borrowed our money to pay for Entitlements for the Rich and Powerful, Republicans showed where their loyalties lie. It is the Rank of Privilege, and it does stink. Phew!

Maintaining the social safety net maintains society. These programs we've paid for must remain solvent.

People who believe in government for the people and by the people need to replace the fiscally irresponsible ones who would whittle away at what we have left. Social Security must be kept whole and shorn up for the future.

That is not enough. There is only one way to start raising the tide for all. The minimum wage needs to be increased. The Australians are way ahead of us on this. I was lucky enough to visit a few years back. At the time, the US dollar was worth $1.06 of the Aussie dollar. The minimum wage there? $16.80. Also, tipping is mostly unheard of there.

Back here in the United States, the minimum is $7.25*, ever since 2009. Cost of living has never been a factor in determining this very important equalizer. The popular amount being talked about now is raising to fifteen dollars per hour. That's a good start. It will still have to be higher in areas where the cost of housing is significantly higher, but by all means, let's start there!

The original minimum wage* enacted in 1938 was twenty-five cents an hour, and it was bumped to thirty cents the next year. It wasn't considered a living wage then, just the minimum. Today's minimum won't get you very far here in Seattle where I live, the net earnings from that wouldn't cover basic rent. Different areas have to have different standards; that is just how it is here in these far-flung states.

At fifteen dollars per hour, people can start to get a more positive outlook on their prospects. There will always be the naysayers claiming the economy will crash. It won't. Fast food will be pricier, but more people will be able to afford it. Our effort is to raise the tide. Everyone will have to adjust to some things being higher priced. While in Australia, I thought restaurant pricing to be a little higher than here in the states, but there wasn't any tipping, so it was, in effect, less.

*From the US Dept. of Labor Wage and Hour Division

22. "If you don't like the weather, wait five minutes."
     Everyone says that

What about climate change? There will always be naysayers who will refuse to believe we have to do anything about it or that we couldn't possibly have any effect on it or that it will cost jobs. These same naysayers will be the first to complain about how the government didn't do anything about it when Miami gets inundated.

Ninety-nine point nine percent of scientists and meteorologists know we contribute to it and that temperatures have been rising around the globe. Fox News can always find a few who will claim it is all just hysteria. There are also people who believe the world is flat. Dealing with climate change will cost money, but that will create more jobs.

Waiting until coastal cities are being swamped to stop and think about what to do would be addressing the problem too late. Where I used to work, dealing with catastrophic building issues was a common theme since deferred maintenance abounded. It always costs more to deal with catastrophe than when properly prepared with good planning.

As a planetary team we have not done enough. It's never too late to start turning things around. The Trillion Tree Initiative would go a very long way toward reaching the goal of mitigating the carbon already in the atmosphere. Cutting back on the entrenched coal and oil industries is a current sticking point. Having a "carbon tax," such as five cents a gallon on gas and diesel to plant and water trees, puts the money right where it would do the most good. Trees would be a…tremendous planetary wide benefit. Some say this wouldn't accomplish anything. Doing nothing won't accomplish anything.

Solar and wind power are already competitive price wise at delivering energy. Now we need to aggressively work towards installing more of these systems. More jobs! Efforts must be made to put these jobs in the regions that have lost out on the tech explosion. Coal country should be a beneficiary. Make it a win-win.

Climate change naysayers need to be voted out of office. They are right when they say it will cost money to address it. It costs even more to address it after you're already under water. Addressing it now means staving off the worst of it and…More Jobs! These are the jobs that should be encouraged, now. Creating jobs to counter climate change will not break the bank. It will spread the wealth.

We do have the means to turn back climate change. Accepting responsibility is the first step. Implementing changes to reduce carbon output follows. Planting trees draws a circle around it. I do look forward to the daily planting report—ten thousand trees were planted today—for instance. That would be good news to look forward to everyday. Let's create jobs and cut down carbon!

23. "Congress shall make no law respecting an estab-
lishment of religion…" Beginning of the First
Amendment of the constitution

Religious beliefs have been referred to in this compilation. Raised in a Christian church myself, I do count myself as a Christian. However, using religious beliefs as a reason to discriminate against fellow humans can't be allowed, be it race, religion, or lifestyle. It stands among the religions which recognize the same God, that God created us all. Did God make a mistake for us to pass judgement upon? No. Judgement is to be relegated for after we've lived out our lives.

Live and let live. It is not for us to judge. Letting people practice their religion doesn't mean they can discriminate against others. Cast not the first stone. We are all in this thing called life together. Pointing out and decrying our differences won't make the world a better place.

Nazi Germany made a point of wiping out hundreds of thousands, Jewish, and more, the hate which drove that has before and since wiped out many hundreds of thousands more. Hey, we need our differences. Who's going to run our 7-11s on Fridays, Saturdays, and Sundays?

The First Amendment of the Constitution states we can't establish religion(s) through law. Of course, at the time they were thinking only in terms of Christian religions since many came to these shores to practice their own version. Free exercise of religion can in no way include discrimination of LGBTQ+ people or anyone different from yourself in any way or form.

Judge not lest ye be judged. In the final analysis, people need to be allowed their own lifestyle. We are all equal in the eyes of God. A parable tells us to leave the flock to find the lost sheep, not to hunt it down with pitchforks and torches. From now on, when the question of race comes up in a form, I'll check the "other" box and write, "Human."

24. The Foot Soldiers of America, Our Freedom
     Fighters

At this time, a shout out to those of us who have served and those who
now serve in Our National Forces! Thank you so much for all you do
and have done. We are thankful war has been kept off our shores and
we've been provided security from invasion. It is no small task. We
should thank our soldiers whenever we see them. They deserve our
thanks and praise for their sacrifices.

The women and men of our fighting forces do not have it easy. The
needs of our soldiers do not end with their conscription. Mentally and
physically, they need better care than they have received. The Veterans
Health Administration is woefully underfunded.

Suicide rates in the military far exceed civilian. Mental health care
is far underrated in the general population, but for our service people,
it's even worse. It is a disgrace that we've put more money into fewer
hands and let the mental and physical needs of those who serve and
have served onto the rubble pile of Congressional Undersight.

Yes, there are many conflicts in which we have engaged that have
turned off public support. Oil wars will never be popular when there
is so much human suffering in the world. That shouldn't stop us from
taking care of our own who have put their lives on the line to keep us

far from the suffering too much of the rest of the world must endure.

The stories of veterans waiting to get healthcare have got to stop. If the VA can't help them, then they should be able to get their healthcare outside of that system without unnecessary red tape. They should be given front-of-the-line privileges wherever they go for healthcare. Their suffering should not be exacerbated by the military and government failing to fund armed forces aftercare.

Bottom line, military expenses should include healthcare during duty and once all duty is complete. War is hell. Recovery shouldn't be a battle.

25. "If you can't explain it to a six-year-old, you don't understand it yourself." – Albert Einstein

It can't be expressed too much, the importance of teaching children between one and five years old. Elevating the country is tied to education and that begins in those very early years. The sooner we get children into learning, the farther we'll go as a nation.

All licensed daycare centers should have an early childhood education specialist. All children should get licensed daycare. Providing daycare to all children should be a national priority. Giving all kids a great head start will make US a better society. The Naysayers will naturally balk at paying for such a thing. That investment will pay benefits far greater than the cost.

Once kids are in grade school, the ones which need free breakfast/lunch are identified and provided for. This practice must be extended to the critical early years. No one can learn when they're malnourished. We currently have plenty of food in this country to feed everyone. Let's make it happen.

There are children of all races who are undernourished, though blacks have the greatest percentage of poverty of all. This idea of providing essential food for the youngest of our youth may by itself end the cycle of poverty which is so prevalent in the underprivileged.

Essential food and education go hand in hand. We can make this happen. The stock answer when the Child Haters scream about paying for this should be, "Why do you want to hold back the children in our country?" Nutrition and education are linked. Studies prove this. Let's close this link up and make it work together.

Delivering on this promise of food and education will take work. The cycle of poverty won't end overnight, and some who have been trapped in it may not even see the benefit it would bring. If there is a nation that could feed and educate the children, that would be US.

This is going all in to raise the tide. You can't think when you're hungry. Let's feed the minds and bodies. It will make the whole thing click together. Education levels the field for everyone. Everyone deserves a chance to succeed. With that success, continuing innovation will follow; the cycle of poverty can end.

26. The Party to End All Parties…Some Food for
    Thought

There is just no getting around it these days. The Party to End All Parties is the Republican Party. He who would be King says he shouldn't be limited to two terms. Gerrymandering districts to create out of proportion majorities has created a monster. Unilaterally reducing the voter's rolls in several states. This is today's Republican Party.

If you think the two-party system stinks, The Elephants have a big pile solution for you, One Party! Very, very distressing. Allowing the Tweeter-in-Chief to continue flouting the laws he's been asked to uphold and justifying it? Where has the integrity gone? It's lost somewhere in their self-help book.

The Top Mongrel has preached the praises of Putin, Erdogan, and Kim Jong-un. He longs to achieve what they have, a totalitarian pinnacle from which he can't be removed. With their ethos running on a lack of fumes, somehow the Republican Faithful believe they must prop up this megalomaniac to maintain their grip on power.

Their Religion of No Taxes and No Government has morphed into a complete power grab unlike any seen in this Democracy. Since it is a religion to them, they see it as a natural progression for the country to move to. They don't want Democracy; it no longer suits their belief system.

Unfortunately, the people who are fooled all the time have fallen right in step. It's not the first time in the world's history that people have rallied behind a hate-mongering leader. Can people imagine actually having to work for Donald the First? No. Would they want to go to work every day with this boss to terrorize them? No. Would they want him in charge of the business they work for? No, especially since his businesses fail. They wouldn't think twice about jumping ship if they were in his crew, as many have already done.

His Lordship commands no respect. It's hard to give respect to one who shows such an absolute disregard for all that work for him. He keeps a fleet of buses to throw everybody under. Except he does like Putin, Erdogan, and Kim Jong-un since they have what his heart desires—absolute power.

There can be no excuse to show devotion to someone so devoid of human compassion. His only passion is the constant feeding of his overblown ego. The word "I" emanates from his mouth constantly in the barrage of self-congratulations over achievements which he imagined. Self-love oozes from his very soul, and he's not ashamed to admit it. It is his only love…

Well, enough about He Who Would Be King. The only solution to returning true Democracy to our country is to get out there and vote. The more who vote, the better. At this juncture, you must already know how important your vote is. Go out there and get more folks to vote.

Vote, vote, vote, vote, vote. Every time. Let's make sure there are three certain things in life, Death, Taxes, and Voting!

27. "Vote early and often." A phrase first popularized
    in the mid-1800s

With low voter turnout, majority outcomes are easier for minority groups. This is one of those things worth repeating. Thirty-five percent of the voting public will always vote "No Taxes, No Government." For the government to be successful, the people running it should believe in government in the first place. Simple, No Taxes, No Government types will never be able to enact laws which can better the country; they-don't-want-to-pay-for-anything.

Getting people to vote at all primary and general elections would be a great leap for Democracy. To encourage voter participation, I'd like to see a tax credit for the primary and general elections every year. Incentivize voting.

Ensuring that every eligible voter is on the list should be tackled by each state. Motor-voter registration is one way to accomplish this. Library cards should include the option for automatic enrollment. Heck, credit card companies can get in on the action, maybe Amazon! Some way to insure everyone has a chance.

There also must always be a paper trail. Electronic balloting can be too easily hacked, and there is no paper trail. If the electronic machine prints out the ballot for the voter to look at before placing it in a separate ballot box where the paper ballots are counted, that can possibly work.

Relying on polling places open only certain hours limits people. Not everyone gets to take two hours off early to make it to the polling station. Hearing about polling stations closing with long lines out the door at the 2018 elections was very distressing. People deserve to get their vote in.

Having a system of total mail-in voting gives people the best chance to be counted. Every state should put that to their voters to allow mail-in voting, giving about two weeks before election day. The ballots should include free postage, but there should always be places where ballots can be placed securely that is accessible to people. Having worked at the post office for two years, I know things get lost in the mail.

Does your state or commonwealth allow for initiatives or referendums by the people? It should. In the state of Washington, some may say there is a plague of them. If you have this power in your state or commonwealth, get a paper mail-in ballot on your ballot! Make Democracy easier to participate in. The more participants, the merrier! The more that vote, the more the heart of America can show. Show heart, show love! Vote! Do it for you; do it for everyone!

28.   Consequences of Our Purchases

Let's get back to job creation. Jobs don't just appear out of nowhere, and they must be paid for. They say Business creates jobs, but
in reality, the money for all those jobs comes right out of our pockets.
We pay someone else to create the jobs, but we pay for them. You vote
for the products you want by how you spend your paycheck. We create
the ever-changing economy.

Let's get creative about the jobs we have. How about becoming
the new primary source of "rare earth" minerals? Sure, it would be easy
to go about it the old-fashioned way by digging into the earth. We
might not be as cheap a source due to our labor costs and environmental standards, but there is a market out there for environmentally
friendly products.

Right now, we have a great supply of these products already that
we don't have to go underground for. It's in our trash. Unimaginably
huge piles of cell phones, VCRs, TVs, and an endless list of electronics
we can recover this stuff called "rare earth." So far, we've been shipping
it away and paying other countries to send it back to us again in
another product. We're already paying for this recycling in one way. A
different way would be to pre-tax the endless list of electronics we buy
every day.

A ten-dollar fee built into a basic TV would certainly be manageable. Twenty-five dollars for the average smart phone? It could be done. We pay for the trash one way or the other; why not create new jobs recycling it right here in the USA? Keep it clean, market it as such; who knows, maybe produce the next batch of electronics here at home. It can be done.

Returning manufacturing back to the US would be great in so many ways. Being dependent on other countries to produce the goods we need to maintain our position as a leader in innovation is a little sketchy. At some point you need to wonder who's the leader and who's being led. We need to bring manufacturing back to make sure we don't lose that skill. We need it back to ensure our own standards are being met.

Once upon a time when you bought an appliance it was expected to be around for another thirty years. Now we're not buying products; the products are just being rented. It might seem to be a reasonable choice to buy, throw away, and buy again because it's so cheap. Do you not grow weary of having to buy a thing time after time?

I bought a small, folding, mustache-trimming pair of scissors over twenty years ago. It is made of stainless steel and was made in the USA. It still is quite sharp. You can't find that now. Stainless steel products made here have all but disappeared. Let's bring them back.

Sure, you can get some small item for three bucks, use it a relatively short while, then throw it out when it under-performs, go out, and throw away another three bucks. How about it gets made with pride in the USA, you pay twelve bucks and never throw it away? Let's opt for scenario two. Less waste, more jobs for us, and the money stays here. You would rather the money stays here, right?

Let's not become a third-world country depending on the rest of the world to produce the hard goods we need to get through our daily lives. It could go that way. Bring manufacturing back home! I have saved a lot of money for the last number of years looking for an item to be made in the USA. Not finding it, I did without. Amazing what you can do without when you control your shopping urges.

Look at labels. Where is the item made? There may be a country you should avoid sending your money to altogether. Pay attention—get value for your money.

29. "Get some rest. If you haven't got your health, then you haven't got anything." Count Rugen to Prince Humperdinck in *The Princess Bride*

It's time the US joined the rest of the industrialized world and had universal healthcare. With a little imagination, we can do it best of all. As previously mentioned, we already outspend the closest "competitor" by over 20 percent per person. That's just the closest one. Our outcomes? We're living shorter lives now than we did twenty years ago and overall health is worse.

Scrapping the one hundred thousand different insurance plans that are out there comes first. The multitude of plans make for small groups which have no weight when it comes to negotiating coverages and pricing. Putting us all into One Group gives us leverage which can't be ignored. There are decisions that just can't be left to those making profit on people's health.

Case in point: The EpiPen. One day it's one price. Next day it costs six times as much. Companies do need to stay in business, and those providing necessary items and drugs need to stay afloat but charging excessive prices for needed items is not making an honest buck. With the power of One Voice, we can get competitive pricing on care and prescriptions.

Some folks are already outsourcing their personal prescriptions to Canada. There are better prices up there; they have National Health! Why have we fallen so far behind on this from our northern neighbor? For one, the Drug Companies have conscripted Congress to help them maintain price fixing by allowing them to keep their monopolies on certain drugs so they can't go generic here.

Those that worry Socializing Medicine will bring the foundations of our great country tumbling to the ground are blowing hot air. National Health is about National Health; let's make it a common interest instead of letting insurance companies divide and conquer the market. Piecemealing us with one hundred thousand plans dilutes our best interests. Single Payor gives us One Voice and takes away the control of our health from the corporate boardroom.

C'mon, get on board with the Single Payor notion. We can get much better care if we put our health into the hands of our doctors and nurses. We already pay for healthcare, one way or the other. Let's put our dough to the best use and save money at the same time. Yes, this will have to be paid for, but small bites can help us with that.

A spoonful of sugar is a start. Once, there was rumor that if a well-known burger franchise raised their prices on a burger five cents, they could cover health insurance for all employees. What if all hamburger had a ten-cent a pound premium on it thrown in at the source so we don't "see" it at the checkout? That wouldn't break the bank, but it could raise a lot towards covering the bills. It could primarily be earmarked for cholesterol and heart issues. The meat packers already have accountants that can handle that paperwork.

How much money could we raise on a penny a pill at the pharmacy or for over the counter meds? It staggers the imagination.

They Who Wish to Pay For Nothing will balk at this sort of talk. Taxes will send markets reeling! Chicken Little will fall in! Wait, what? In the great state of Washington, vice taxes are just about the highest there are. We probably have the top prices for cigarettes and liquor. These industries are not suffering here. Taxing sugar and meat seems appropriate for covering some healthcare costs. We already cough it up for health anyway, but we're not getting full value for what we pay.

Small bites make it easier. Spreading out the cost just makes it simpler. Complaining about paying for things won't take the bills away. Relieving everyone of concern over covering medical bills will take away stress that torments millions. That alone could alleviate a significant number of mental health issues. Which, by the way, need coverage also, as well as dental and vision.

So, c'mon! Let's get together with our doughnuts and cheeseburgers and eat our way to the best Universal Healthcare on the planet! We'll certainly be needing it if we eat like that every day!

30. "…all Citizens United did was to level the playing field for corporate speech." Mitch McConnell (from endcitizensunited.org)

The original framers of the constitution never intended for Big Business to have any semblance of control over elections.The original Citizens United lawsuit brought before the Supreme Court was about allowing a company to be able to run a movie about Hillary Clinton near to an election that had previously been determined to be campaign material as opposed to a "documentary" or an independently produced theater release.

The 5-4 decision which became rendered went further than that, unilaterally allowing any amount of money and resources to be spent on any campaign, unrestricted by previous laws, so that the poor Big Businesses could compete on an equal level to the common voter.That is like having a T-ball player competing with Babe Ruth.

How is it possible to justify Big Money's right to outspend those who can barely afford to throw their dollars into the mix? This was a colossal miscarriage of justice(s).It is a frightening robbery of common citizens of their ability to have equal say in what constitutes an elective campaign.The 1 percent and corporate America have more money than the 99 percent.We have been taken out of the equation.

The signs are now all out there. The One-Party System now has the tool needed to dominate the political scene. They Who Would Be Fooled All the Time are already bought in despite the lack of benefit in it for them personally because they have accepted the religion of "No Taxes, No Government." The fervor will sustain them even in the face of mounting facts.

Overturning Citizens United will only come about by electing those who believe government can work for people to make this a better country. The "Mine, mine, mine" mentality will not lead to common good. It has only led to fewer people with more of the money. Today I read in the Seattle Times that Amazon was spending over a million dollars on city of Seattle races. Is that leveling the playing field?

Big Business doesn't need any government handouts. They're BIG already. Small business needs life support, that's where most the jobs are, after all. Small farmers need life support. The independent farmers are being plowed under by Mega-Agriculture. Let's level the playing field for people, small businesses, and farms.

31.   Competing with BIG BUSINESS

Small businesses are hard pressed to compete with the Big Boys. The Big Boys have resources. They can subsidize a semblance of health insurance that the little ones are hard pressed to afford. What if there was Universal Health? Suddenly, small businesses could find it easier to keep good help. The lure of better benefits wouldn't be so material.

There are many communities out there who thought Walmart would be so handy to have in the neighborhood. Then those communities lost their friendly neighborhood pharmacist or local grocery store. They thought, "Oh, but the jobs!", then found maybe they wouldn't get enough hours to qualify for benefits. They may have also found the products being sold were just rentals. So cheap! Just buy another if it breaks or fails.

The above scenario has played out enough that many communities are fighting back to retain their small-town feel, Walmart has been kept at bay. The dream of the cheap expansive shopping experience has diminished in the eyes of the smaller communities. Good for them!

It was tough enough for small business when the Mega-Retailers would move in. Now, even the Mega Stores are closing up shop because Amazon has revolutionized the shopping experience! I haven't bought into that particular revolution; it seems more of a shakedown like an offer that can't be refused.

Shopping in jammies is okay when you're looking for replacement filters or a book. Being able to look over hard goods, checking where they're made, see the quality, verify the fitting, and knowing you won't have to send it back is far more fulfilling. Your local retailer would agree.

Get out in your own neck of the woods and find the pleasures of shopping in your neighbor's store. You just might be surprised at what you find.

32. "I have always depended on the kindness of strangers." Blanche DuBois in *A Streetcar Named Desire*

Lost amid the yelling and screaming is that we do need the help of strangers to make it through every day. Building walls on the borders or in our minds can't keep out the fact we all rely on people we don't know and whom we'll never meet.

Did I hear someone shout and say, "I don't need anyone's help; I can do it all myself." Unless you're living off the grid somewhere, growing your own food or subsisting on fish, wild game and gathering wild food off the land, you are dependent on other people. Even if you're a hunter-gatherer, you've probably got some manufactured tool or cooking implement to get you through your day.

The list of people upon whom we draw to get us to the end of the day goes on and on. Just for the food in the refrigerator or pantry, there are hundreds, if not thousands, of people needed to grow, harvest, process, transport, display, and sell at the grocery store. Then the people who made your car or bus and provided the petrol must be counted.

If you ever drive up and down I-5 from Seattle to the Mexican border, you'll see and likely pass hundreds of trucks bringing innumerable daily necessities to your home or energy provider. It's pointless to count how many we rely on who also rely on us. We are all in this together.

Pointing out differences between each other accomplishes nothing. It distracts from getting needed things done. Race, religion, ethnicity, regional affiliation, or gender identity do not make us better or worse than the next person. The Declaration of Independence states we are all created equal. Unfortunately, we're still litigating that.

For us to move forward, we must embrace the differences. Recognizing everyone has strengths and weaknesses and working with those to make the whole greater than the sum is what will bring us greater achievement. Creating divisiveness leads only to stagnation not accomplishment.

We have to work together. It is essential for society to put aside differences and recognize we do need each other, because we do. Let's call it the Declaration of Interdependence.

33. "Pay attention and attention will pay you back."
...might be mine...

Equal pay for equal work. That's absolutely fair. Women certainly get the short end of that stick, though. Minorities, too. Out in the working world, varying jobs get a wide range of pay, not necessarily based on value. One job which deserves greater pay is teaching. Education is the most important thing society can do for itself.

Every year many leave the field of education because of lack of pay. Frustration plays a part, but that comes with many jobs. Proper compensation would go a long way towards keeping quality educators in our schools and mitigating their frustration. Recruiting and retaining good teachers would truly benefit the entire country.

Currently, computer programmers right out of college can get paid more than the highest teacher salary—after thirty years in the classroom with a master's in education. We are not paying attention to the value of a good education. Everyone wants their kid to do well in school; well, some parents are satisfied if their child just graduates from high school. All good.

We need to recognize that giving our children the best possible education will advance the country as a whole. The best education will come from properly motivated teachers, ones who feel they will be able to afford a home if they stay the course. Ones that won't feel left behind by their peers in the Pursuit of Happiness.

Many excellent teachers leave because they simply are paid better at any number of other jobs. Educating our up and coming generations is the single most important thing we do as a society. It should be compensated as such. Paying for a good education should not have to be a negotiation issue every three years or however long each contract is.

Hurray for those who chose to remain as educators! It is a challenging job, whether you're working with first graders, middle school, or high school students. The parents can be more challenging. Let's give our teachers the pay deserving of the importance of their job.

Charter schools won't cut it; their success rate is no better than the rest. Whatever "innovation" they may say they bring to the table; it is no miracle cure. The additional head scratcher is they don't have to meet the same standards as the regular schools. In the state of Washington, which instituted this albatross through initiative a few years back, we're getting a high rate of failure on the schools that were created.

If we are committed to getting better schools, we should be committed to paying our educators better. They are getting the short end of the stick. Let's improve teacher pay to improve our schools. That's how our education systems will excel. Raise this tide! There is definitely income inequality in education. Our children will benefit from this. Society will benefit and the benefits will outweigh the costs. Teachers deserve better pay.

34. Income Disparity

In 2016 this issue got a bit of traction. Even Republicans brought it up in debates, well, mentioned it. The Federal Minimum Wage hasn't been raised since July 2009. Over ten years now. The only way to start to combat Income Disparity is to raise the minimum wage. It stands at $7.25 an hour. However many who work for that wage, it's way too many.

Some cities and states have already increased that. Seattle breached the fifteen-plus dollars per hour as well as other cities. When the overall minimum is raised to fifteen dollars, these other localities will have to raise theirs again, too. It will not cause economic ruin, though there will be an adjustment period, mentally as well as fiscally.

The biggest change initially will be in the cost of going out to eat. That will take some getting used to, but more people will be able to afford to go out to eat! Yes, I think this will be a win for restaurants, even though costs will go up. The Australians have already bested us on this one for many years. They are nearly at twenty dollars per hour, and this has been rising with the cost of living for many years.

Fifteen dollars an hour is the start. It needs to be automatically indexed. We shouldn't need continual acts of Congressional whim to keep the populace out of poverty. The current minimum is poverty. A living wage makes it possible for everyone to hope for a chance to get ahead.

Any job that needs to be paid for is an essential job. Whether it's pushing a broom, bussing tables, providing medical care, or washing windows. All jobs are essential. Coupled with National Healthcare, things will look rosier for everyone.

After the Bush Recession began in 2007, a lot of people lost good paying jobs which never got replaced. Houses were repossessed. The economy has looked good on paper since 2009, but many of those who were compromised back then never recovered. It's time we righted the ship and raised the tide for all to benefit.

Bumping up the minimum will bring only a temporary adjustment to how the economy runs. The benefits will outweigh whatever short term inconveniences are experienced. The greater bulk of jobs are already over the minimum. I can tell you the Aussies are happier than Americans as a group. They're being paid better. When I visited five years ago, their minimum was $16.80. People seemed happy at their jobs.

Let's make people happier with their jobs here. It won't break the bank. The Naysayers will cry, "There will be economic ruin!" There won't be. It will help level the field. Pride in occupation will increase. Motivation will be enhanced. The start of the new, improved, Era of Trickle Up, will have begun!

35. "…to make ample provision for the education of all children residing within its borders." Article IX, Section 1 of the Washington State Constitution—thanks Wikipedia

Education is the most important thing we offer our children—and adults!—for the continued success of our country. Paying for this will always pay dividends, for competing in the world marketplace, the betterment of society and our way of life.

Education is job one and begins on day one. As previously noted, a child's brain development is most critical in their first five years of life. As a society, we need to insure everyone can receive the tools necessary in their early years to be able to compete on this increasingly difficult planet. This is where we can truly provide a level playing field.

Daycare is an issue for all working adults, even stay-at-home parents. All children should have access to daycare, and daycare should provide learning opportunities throughout the day. This would include providing proper education for daycare workers so they can best help mold this young and exuberant population.

Just as students in K-12 are identified as needing free meals, we need to identify the preschoolers who need good nourishment. You can't think straight on an empty stomach, after all. Development of sound mind and body go hand in hand. Feeding the body fuels the brain. We need to ensure this happens.

There will be those who will complain about paying for all this. It's already being paid for by most people anyway. We just need to cover the rest. In the long run, as wages equalize, there will be fewer folks on public assistance. Early education will be the bedrock for the end of the cycle of poverty.

We don't need massive institutions full of small children. Small daycare in every neighborhood works best for all. Supporting the small daycare with education for those who work with the kids is essential. A trained and reasonably paid work force is necessary for our kids in their formative years.

Once again, the benefit of having all children get access to quality daycare outweighs the cost. This is a long-term investment in the country's future. Our future is dependent on the way we raise our kids. Let's give all of them the tools needed to succeed in life.

Leaving no child behind is a great concept. One day they will be our leaders and giving all of them a solid education will create greater diversity. We need our future leaders to know how to do higher math so they keep their budgets balanced. It may also be time to have our elective representatives required to pass a high school math exam with algebra. We don't want to leave our legislators behind.

36. Climate Change

Way back in the 1970s, climate change was spoken of, but the concept couldn't get traction in the popular perception. Times have changed greatly on this. Now, somewhere along 99.9 percent of scientists agree that not only is it happening but we unsuspecting humans have drastically contributed to this.

Fox News and certain conservative leaders (is that what they are?) have found a few scientists you can count on your hand that will disavow this. Or, they say it will cost jobs. Au contraire, jobs will be created by addressing climate change as soon as possible. What do you think is cheaper—preventing the flood or cleaning up afterward? This is not a trick question.

We are already working towards clean energy options to supply our homes. The cost of this clean energy is already competitive with "traditional" sources. These "traditional" sources, oddly enough, receive billions in government support. The consequences of "traditional" energy haven't been properly quantified to account for all costs related to their production. If those costs were added to the equation, then "traditional" energy is more expensive that clean energy.

Small bites are the easiest to swallow. A simple five-cent-a-gallon tax on gasoline and diesel can go to planting back the trees we've been cutting down for thousands of years. This would be a carbon tax that goes directly to reducing carbon in the air. Let's hear it for the Trillion Tree Initiative! Yes, some will say this would be a waste of time and energy, but it won't be a waste. Even if we stopped all carbon production now, it would take over a hundred years for it all to dissipate to "normal" levels. We need to take every step we can to eliminate carbon in the air. Trees will do this for us while pushing back the desertification we've been creating for millennia.

Other carbon taxes can go to implementing clean energy projects. Small bites work for that, too. We already pay for everything; let's pay for carbon reduction. If the cost is built into the source, it comes out as a much smaller figure. Also, clean energy production should be instituted in the regions which have been most affected by the high cost associated with coal.

Appalachia has been disproportionately hurt by both the decline of coal as well as the Bush Recession. They have still not recovered from that, ten years later, despite the job rate numbers indicating a robust economy. Job creation has bypassed this region, by and large, during the long period of growth since 2009. It isn't the only area which has failed to gain traction since then.

Small bites tacked on to the overall cost of an item evens out the burden. Sure, the energy companies will balk at anything which comes out of their bottom line. They have the accountants already to handle the paperwork. They will still pull down profits as always, any carbon tax will barely move the needle on their stock options and be pennies on the dollar to us.

The time has come to aggressively address climate change. We are all responsible, and we can all play a part. Jobs will be created by dealing with this, not destroyed, as advertised by the disbelievers. The jobs created will be good paying and clean. Putting people to work cleaning up carbon invests in our future.

37. No [one] shall be compelled to frequent or sup-
     port any religious worship or ministry or shall
     otherwise suffer on account of [their] religious
     opinions or beliefs." From another quote of
     Thomas Jefferson

The world is ten thousand years old. Just kidding. That is how some would literally interpret the Bible. Another explanation can clarify this. Just as a day on Earth is different from a day on any other given planet, a day on Earth is hardly a blip in the course of time in the universe. I offer this, as example, originally humor but possible fable, as paraphrased by me:

A destitute soul wanders the back alleys of Seattle pondering the mysteries of the universe. Gazing up at the heavens through the skyscrapers, this person wonders aloud, "Lord, what is a million years to you?". Amazed, this response is heard from above, "Why, a million years is like a minute to me." Stunned at this our brave soul speaks another question, "What is a million dollars to you?" The reply, "Why, a million dollars is like a dollar to me." Turning the empty pockets of their pants out, another question blurts out, "Lord, could you give me a dollar?" The answer comes readily, "Certainly, child, in a minute."

Time is relative. Just ask Einstein. This holds true for the universe. The Hubble Telescope has…unearthed many wonders across the currently known universe. One thing appears certain—the universe has been around for eons. We are a speck in that universe. The Bible has been written by a known error prone group we know as humans. Some literalness needs to be taken with a grain of salt.

Despite everyone's right to believe in their particular religious doctrines, no one has a right to push their doctrine down onto everyone else. Discrimination in the name of religion cannot be tolerated.

Knowing the discussion of religion makes for a touchy subject; let's just go on about science, which has a multitude of adherents as well as the scofflaws of physics. There are many groups who denounce science, who would, in fact, prefer not to have it taught in schools. They may also have a very rudimentary understanding of math.

Science is nothing without math. Math has been calculated to deliver men to the moon, determine how satellites can fly around the Earth or stationery in orbit. It is a fabulous tool in constructing buildings, bridges, and machines that can fly! Science has grown out of math. There are still many mysteries to unearth.

Please, learn to embrace science. It may not have solved all our problems in coming to terms with day to day life, but it has brought us medicine, the ability to communicate in an instant, longer and healthier lives, and a passable understanding of Ikea instructions.

For those of you who may insist science is just thrown at us by white smocked geeks using nonsensible gobbledygook to explain climate change, I have this request; please put your cell phone down while driving.

38.   What About Social Security?

The average person is not a financial wizard. I know, I've met us. The creation of Social Security was a fabulous method to help people survive in their dotage. As it was setup, it was never intended to be the sole income that would take care of all your needs in retirement. The intention was to be a reliable base on which you could depend.

There are forces at work which want to take away this guarantee. They cannot be allowed to succeed. Personally, taking from the fortunes of those who voted to raid this nest egg for other purposes would be a good place to start in the replenishment of the fund, however unlikely that is to occur.

Keeping the system whole and self-sufficient can be done. The math has already been applied to addressing this. One way would be to simply separate out from the outlays those items which aren't considered retiree benefits. Those outlays can be sourced elsewhere. Raising the percentages for business and worker tax on income could also be an answer.

Privatization is the trendy solution for the conservative crowd. Privatization is another term for "how can we get a cut on this pile of dough." We already have TSAs, IRAs, 401Ks, etc., which I recommended everyone take advantage of. Those options, though, do not provide a set, reliable income. Only Social Security gives us the peace of mind of a steady paycheck. It's a keeper.

Since most of us aren't CPAs or Financial Giants, we aren't best qualified to make consistently good decisions. You can listen to the "experts" and get recommendations, but if you choose to throw all your dough into some currently high-flying fund, it could go belly up later, and then you're done.

You may know people who put savings into penny stocks that no longer exist. There are so many ways to gamble away your retirement. Even investing in the 401s, 403s, IRA, or other sheltered retirement options, you'll never get a steady check you can rely on. Social Security is the fallback reliable income to keep you steady, much like a pension plan.

Ask anyone receiving Social Security today if they would like to see their steady income put into the hands of Private Industry. You won't get too many takers for that offer. The screaming would be loud and clear should Privatization be moved forward. Let's call the whole thing off.

Maybe Congress would ensure the solvency of Social Security if they were forced to live on it. We can have initiatives put on the ballot in our respective states that make congressional retirement pay taxed to correspond to what they would have gotten with Social Security. It makes me smile to think of it. It might light a fire under their collective rear ends.

Referring to Social Security as an entitlement can get a person's dander up. We worked for that! Any Representative who calls it an entitlement needs certain removal from office. You don't want them in charge of your money. They have already demonstrated a lack of understanding of simple mathematics by borrowing money to give to those who already possess great quantities of dough.

If your representative or senator uses the term entitlement, they need to be replaced by a responsible adult. Part of the problem could be they were never properly educated. Perhaps all elected officials should be given a high school math test to see if, by chance, they got left behind. If they don't pass, they can't go on the ballot! They are, after all, in charge of large sums of money and complicated budgets. It's a concept worth enacting – Leave no congressperson behind!

39. Small Bites Revisited

Paying for Universal Healthcare is an issue. At present, healthcare is covered for many through their employer. This money is already in that pipeline. The trick now is to cover the people working for small businesses which can't afford this expense and for the many unfortunates who are unemployed.

The spoonful of sugar tax can go a long way to cover this built-in at the front end of the manufacturing process. Adding ten cents to a cup of sugar won't stop anyone from affording a bag. The Big Sugar processors have accountants who can handle one more line item. It won't throw the commodity markets out of whack. It pinpoints an aspect of food which creates health problems, like diabetes and obesity.

The cost of this would be spread out over thousands of products, but it would just get taken out at the front end instead of a line item at the checkout stand. The manufacturers can make the payments. This won't break their bank. They just pass the cost on, of course. The rest of us don't see the bill, and it would be just pennies on the dollar.

The same thing can be done with meat. If you're spreading out a cost of ten cents per pound across the width and breadth of products and let the Big Processors pay for it up front, us folk at the back end will hardly notice. They're passing on the cost, as always, but their accountants deal with just one more line item. Just another thought on spreading out costs without breaking the bank.

No discussion of sharing health costs would be complete without bringing up the drug companies. Imagine if every pill had a built-in cost of one cent. That would certainly spread out the cost. The math on the result of that may just be over the top. Certainly, the drug companies already employ accountants that can handle one more line item. It certainly targets an item directly related to health. Adding this one cent alone may get over the hump of mental health coverage and dental coverage, which should be included in any discussion of National Healthcare.

Small bites can work! We already know that we pay for everything. It comes with the territory. We pay for all the jobs. We pay for all the materials. We'll always pay for the things we need; it's part of how economies work. We can pay for National Healthcare because we already are! We've only just begun to bite!

40.   Waging War for A Living Wage

Rent in Seattle isn't the highest in the nation, but it's working on it. According to komonews.com, in January of 2019 the average price for a one-bedroom apartment comes to $1,900 per month. Fifteen dollars an hour is currently the minimum wage here. If you do the math, it takes about 126 hours to cover the rent. That is some tough sledding considering there are only 176 working hours in an average full-time month. Hopefully, rent is cheaper in your neck of the woods.

Fifteen dollars an hour is a good start for much of the nation. In other localities and states, it will need to be higher. If the Aussies can pull this off, we certainly can. The In-Heir-Ently Entitled probably long for the good old days of serfdom. Work their land and you get to keep enough food to survive on while they keep the lion's share.

Though we did throw off the House of Lords over two hundred years ago, a New Nobility has arisen to fill that vacuum. Having a population available who can do no better than the currently low minimum wage reminds the New Nobility of those bygone glory days when fiefdoms kept the money in fewer hands. Let's raise the tide.

Trickle up should become the new rage. It starts with a living wage for all. Some parts of your daily living costs may go up, but the bulk of the economy won't be affected because many jobs are already above the fifteen-dollar mark. It won't be an onerous burden to pay somewhat more for some basics. Paying for a healthier economy will pay dividends for everyone.

Most people do want to see those around them thrive and succeed. Making this happen may seem to be brash or bold. They say history favors the bold. Let's be bold and institute a living wage at which ordinary folk can see a way up. Sure, you'll hear the economy will come crashing to a halt. It won't. The economy will adapt. It has always adapted to changing circumstance. Looms replaced handsewn items. Trains replaced wagons. Cars replaced horses. Adapting to change is what we do.

The biggest hit to the economy that ever occurred was during the OPEC oil embargo of the 1970s. One day we were paying twenty-five cents for a gallon of gas, next month it was fifty cents. Energy costs doubled over night! There was some steep inflation after that, but energy is central to the economy. The minimum wage is not central to our economy.

Raising the minimum wage will create a better economy. More people will afford more things. Less people will require public assistance! Coupled with National Healthcare, the entire Nation will experience a boost in their lifestyle. This can really happen! We must go boldly into raising the tide!

We are way behind the Australians in this regard, but we have them to thank for having already implemented this and shown it won't break the bank. Don't let the shrieking "Mine! Mine! Mine!" crowd make you believe it can't work. It can work. It's been proven.

Certain things will go up in price, but it will be relatively small bites. We could possibly do away with tipping. The Aussies already have. We have been on the wrong side of the world on this. Tipping is well ingrained to our collective psyche, so it may die a slow death—all good.

The point is, it's time to raise the tide. We can move proudly into a new age where people have a job that's needed and are compensated for taking care of that job. Raising the tide benefits everyone. Let's reap the benefits. It will be a better harvest.

41. "I am not an advocate for frequent changes in laws and constitutions, but laws and institutions must go hand in hand with the progress of the human mind. As that becomes more developed, more enlightened, as new discoveries are made, new truths discovered and manners and opinion change. With the change of circumstances, institutions must advance also to keep pace with the times. We might as well require a man to wear the coat which fitted him when a boy as civilized society to remain ever under the regimen of their barbarous ancestors." Thomas Jefferson, as written in the Jefferson Memorial

TJ has been one of my favorite revolutionaries. His words still resound today as he could perceive a future far different than his present. He knew what had already been undertaken was a work in progress. Most would agree there is plenty of work still to be done. Agreeing on what constitutes progress will always bring debate.

For about two hundred years, laws were passed to prevent monopolies from taking over industries, keeping competition alive to stimulate more competition. Monopolies were broken up and commerce diversified. Manufacturing continually improved. Even as robots came to dominate the process, new jobs maintaining and programming those robots were created. New jobs, previously unimagined, began to transform modern processes.

In the 1980s a new kind of business began to flourish, but it wasn't about creation. The '80s ushered in the trickle-down theory. High inflation kept home prices down. Businesses and banks failed in large numbers. The new business was buying failed companies, then selling off the assets for a profit, leaving the carcasses of manufacturing plants to sit idle.

Those were hard times. It was during this period that Unions began their precipitous decline. Trickle down was all the rage. Conservatism became trendy. The National Debt went right up, faster than ever before. It was okay! Big Business was thriving! Yes, the business of funneling more money into fewer hands began. History verifies this.

In the '90s, under the Clinton Administration, we paid the debt down for several years running despite the Republican legislative control his last four years in office. George W. Bush took over in 2001, though Al Gore received more popular votes. Bush claimed it was a mandate to reinstitute the trickle-down theory, and again, great deficits were borrowed to funnel the cash to the top income brackets and corporations.

Many things happened during the Bush Administration. At this time, I will limit the discussion to the infamous Enron bankruptcy and the many bank failures which ultimately led to the Bush Recession beginning in 2007. In 2008, the government started to bail out the banking and auto industries.

By the time Obama took office in 2009, deficit spending had horrifically soared, and the Republicans were quick to blame Obama for the sorry state of affairs. He got blamed for the trillion-dollar deficit, but no tax increase was allowed to cover our debts. Incredibly, the economy recovered and grew for over ten years.

Of course, in 2017, in full control of Congress, once again the Republicans invoked their right to borrow more money to give to the already privileged, and our deficits are increasing as the money is further concentrated into the hands of the 1 percent. It seems unfathomable that such fiscal irresponsibility gets rewarded with votes from the general public, but some are fooled all of the time.

Irresponsibility is not a strong enough term. Robbery would be closer to the truth. While we witness bridges falling, water systems failing, and transportation issues, the "No Government" types have patted themselves on the back again for putting the money into fewer hands. There is no trickle down. The record shows the concentration of money is greater than it's ever been.

Someday we hope to elect people who have a firm grasp of simple math and the ethical responsibility to right this inequity. It is time to trend toward real progress and positive change. Let go of those policies which just concentrate the money, because it doesn't trickle down. It's another example of barbarous practices by Tea Party Practitioners, and history will count them among the barbarous.

42. Infrastructure, Infrastructure, Infrastructure

If I said it once, I wouldn't have said it enough; infrastructure is job one. On the primrose path that led to the election of He Who Would Be Emperor, we were told he would take care of infrastructure. It turns out the number one priority was to boost the upper stratosphere of the landed gentry by borrowing more money. Then we were told that our Entitlements, like Medicare, Medicaid, and Social Security needed to be siphoned off to pay for the infrastructure.

Maybe we can just reverse that number one priority and use that to take care of infrastructure. The news has a parade of stories about fallen bridges, failing water systems, and deteriorating roadways. These are things that need immediate attention. These are the jobs we need. There is so much work to be done; it may be hard to get enough people to fill all the jobs.

Let's get started. One of the things that keeps us a leader in industry is a transportation network that lets the goods flow. Maintaining that is essential to our ability to keep pace with the world. Deferred maintenance costs more in the long run. Choosing the low bidder does not guarantee quality work. Cutting back on projects now only costs more down the road. You don't have to look far to find that out.

It behooves us to make good decisions on quality, so we don't have to do it again in twenty years. We should be thinking long term for the best investment of our money. Mass transit to get cars off the road pays dividends. Getting trains to match the speed of those in Europe would be fabulous. You can go from Florence, Italy, to Venice in two hours on a train that can go 180 mph. It takes five hours to drive. Which would you prefer?

Our infrastructure is lagging in quality and maintenance. We need to focus up. The jobs will always be welcome. The "No Taxes, No Government" types will always complain about paying for this. We are a rich country. As long as we don't borrow ourselves into a third world state, we can pay for transportation. It is imperative to build and maintain transportation infrastructure. Gas taxes for this haven't been significantly raised in over fifty years.

Taking care of our water systems is equally important. This isn't a waiting game; safe drinking water can't be ignored. Staying healthy is dependent on good water. Ours crops need water. Water is the greatest commodity we have. Ensuring its safety and accessibility is inseparable from our basic needs.

Some years back, there was a massive blackout across the eastern states. California is now experiencing blackouts. This shouldn't happen. Energy transmission needs reliable networks. Talk about being a third world state; energy blackouts slap us in the face. Now it seems California gets to have blackouts regularly. This-should-not-be-happening!

Deferred maintenance has been a hallmark of the modern conservative. Spend less! Except it just costs more down the line. "Mine! Mine!

Mine!" won't feel very good huddling under the blankets when the power goes out. We do need to be proactive in keeping transmission lines intact, power distribution networks stable, and verifying the safety and integrity of oil and natural gas pipelines.

All this does cost money. Putting off addressing it costs more. The jobs are out there waiting to be made. We can pay for it; there is plenty of dough is this country. There are plenty of people who want good jobs. The economy has been expanding; there is no time like the present to get infrastructure properly taken care of.

Jobs, jobs, jobs!

43. "The More Parties the Merrier" You've heard this before if you've been to college...

The One-Party System discussed earlier would be foisted upon us by the "Grand Old Elephant Dung Party."They have made strides trying to implement this in several states.The great majority of us do not believe in a one-party system, reminiscent of Russia or China. Maybe the One-Party folks could move to one of those countries for us and really try it on for size.

There is a solution to getting away from the two-party system and end gerrymandering for all time. End districting in all the states. Instead of districting, representatives would be allotted for each party based on the number of registered party members. Each party would then vote their respective allotment of reps. Even those who registered as not affiliated could vote for an unaffiliated rep.

The above described system would probably not be the choice the two biggies would opt for, especially the "Dung Party." Suddenly though, should their numbers prove sufficient, other parties would have representation in Congress.The Senate might prove to be a bit more difficult to break through, but eventually smaller voices would be heard.

The concept of gerrymandering would become moot. More voices would infuse the discussions. It would definitely create a politics as unusual from the current state of affairs. Allowing more voices does sound fairer than what's been the standard for so many years. We might even be able to end the deadlock created by what the "I Don't Want to Pay For Anything" set has perpetrated for the last forty years or so.

New ideas could get traction. It is painfully obvious that the same old, same old is not getting the jobs done. Instead of traction we're getting a treadmill, but it seems to be going backward. Like doing the "Moonwalk."

Forward progress appeals to the forward thinking. The present rigor mortis permeating the powers that be brings back to mind Thomas Jefferson's words, "…as civilized society to remain ever under the regimen of their barbarous ancestors." Let's embrace a future where concepts are explored for their efficacy and tested for the benefits they may provide, not limited by someone harping on another line item they just don't want to pay for.

Outcomes are difficult to predict. Discussion should proceed without rancor. We could possibly be merrier with more parties.

44. "The right of citizens of the United States to vote shall not be denied or abridged by the U.S. or any state on account of race, color or previous condition of servitude." Fifteenth Amendment, 1870 – in 1920 the Nineteenth Amendment added sex.

Abridgement of voting rights has become trendy in certain states where the gerrymandering has favored the "Party to End All Parties—but Ours." Clearly, it seems, the intention of the Constitution was to make sure everyone got to exercise their right to vote. Mass elimination of people from the voter rolls has taken place in certain Southeastern States and Wisconsin.

How many Sam Johnsons can there be? Or Robert Smith? John Jones? There can be a lot. Arbitrarily eliminating them from the rolls does not look as an attempt to combat fraud. It appears to be a way of scraping off those who wouldn't vote in the desired way. The "We Need to Be The Only Party" group needs a gut check.

This behavior is tantamount to totalitarianism. Democracy is being mocked. Can we call it "Demockracy?" Race seems to have a lot to do with it. Votes in Georgia were "picked up" and then never dropped off to be counted. Mail-in votes have been ignored. Provisional ballots left unprocessed. People are being robbed of their right to vote.

This must be corrected. Get out and make sure your relatives, friends, and neighbors are registered to vote. This is one thing we do have control of. We can't let it just slip away. Get on the bandwagon. Voting is the thing that separates Democracy from totalitarianism. Make sure we all keep that right.

The more people who vote, the merrier. Better results will come of better participation. Democracy is a participation activity. No one can claim "I'm just not that political" anymore. We have seen there are forces at work who would wrest Democracy from our hands.

Voting should be easier, and there should always be a paper trail. Electronics can't be trusted; all votes need to be traced back to paper. It's the only way of assuring the veracity of the results.

An all-mail-in ballot, sent at least two weeks prior to an election, would give everyone ample opportunity to vote. No more lines at some far-off polling locale. Postage included makes it even better. Allowing drop off sites for those who might prefer to drop it off without relying on the post office should be an option.

Get out and encourage participation. Voting is not only a right, it's a duty to yourself and our fellow country folk. Do your duty. Be dogged. Don't drop the bag. Vote every time. And get your friends, relatives, neighbors, and loved ones out there, too.

45. Leveling the New Age of Communication

There is another aspect to this new age of communication which needs addressing. First, a discussion on land line telephones, which do still exist. Some one hundred or so years ago it was determined everyone had the right to be able to get telephone service and that everyone should have the same payment options no matter if they lived in the big city or miles off some country road.

It was considered a universal standard to allow people anywhere to stay in contact, and it was a deemed a safety issue so folks could alert police, medical, or fire assistance no matter where they lived. Like the post office, it was a lifeline which we all got to be connected with and not have to pay more just because we lived off the beaten path.

Now here we are, and though access to landlines hasn't gone away, use of landlines is dropping off daily as people don't want to pay for two phones. So we are in a situation where, yes, you can still make landline calls out in the boonies, but landlines are now old technology. Cell phones have replaced landlines, but coverage is far from complete.

If you live a mile off the nearest road, you may still maintain your landline. Once you've left the house, though, there may not be coverage for another twenty miles. This new tech hasn't reached out and permeated the land like telephone wire has. This new tech needs to be stretched out across the nation equally for the same reasons landlines were legislated to go where the people are. It's a safety issue.

Recognizing it is the new universal standard, we must build the network out to cover everyone. Cell phones are in almost everyone's hands now, child to adult. I live in the big city, a high-tech hub, and service is spotty in my neighborhood. This must be addressed nation-wide. Guess what—more jobs!

Building out to every remote wilderness is not what we're after here. Just cover where people live and maybe include the main visitor hubs in the National Parks; my phone doesn't seem to work there.

Just as the landline was considered the standard of the day, cell service must be considered today's standard. You may have heard certain politicians whining about "those poor people complaining about their situations while holding a cell phone in their hand" as if only the privileged should be considered worthy to possess a luxury item like a cell phone.

That sort of attitude displays a lack of recognition of modern times. Cell phones are the means by which people everywhere are now communicating. Catch up to the times. What sort of dinosaur would say such a thing? It's time to level this playing field, also.

Keeping up in the twenty-first century means having a cell phone. It has become the new standard even if some choose not to see it. Ensuring equal access is as important for this now as landlines were back in the old twentieth century.

46.   "I Saw It on The Internet" We've all heard this

Speaking of Modern Times, availability of the internet is another issue which has become a sticky point between the haves and have nots. Computer and internet access issues have made the gap between the haves and have not even greater. This must also be equalized.

There are any number of children out there who can't compete on the same level because of quality computer and internet access. In the future, after a Living Wage has been instituted, this problem could go away. Currently, we have disparity out there to be corrected so all children can compete in our schools on equal footing.

After school computer lab availability needs to be provided. Yes, good education costs money, but consider the cost of ignorance. If the intent is to leave no child behind, equal access to computers and the internet must be part of the equation. Computer skills are no longer an option; it's a requirement.

Computers seem ubiquitous, but not all children are fortunate enough to have regular access. We must take care to give all children this fundamental right to receive a modern education.

Providing Wi-Fi internet in certain neighborhoods may get us closer to achieving internet equality. Our phone, internet, and cable TV bills have a lot of taxes thrown in them. Is any of that going to helping equalize internet access for all? It should.

Internet access in the here-and-now needs to also be provided, just like telephones in the days of yore, as it has become another integral link in keeping us all connected. FCC rules should apply for internet access as they did for telephones because that is now the dominant technology.

If you're a fan of more jobs, this will keep us busy for a while. It will provide well-paying jobs. Jobs that will help provide equal access. It might also provide a lot of cat videos, but not everything is 100 percent efficient.

47. "Voting with Your Pocketbook" A recurring theme

You must have heard of this, voting with your pocketbook. It works. Would you like to promote American Made goods? Look for it on the label. Keep looking until you find it. You'll save money in the meantime, because it is harder to find things Made in America.

A lot of manufacturers have moved operations offshore. This will bite us in the rear in the long run if we lose the ability to produce basic items right here at home. We should be willing to pay more to keep our own folk gainfully employed. Getting better quality goods is always worth extra. You do get what you pay for.

Just twenty years ago it was much easier to find things, Made in America. Seeing a Union Label assured us there was pride in the manufacture. Purchases lasted longer, worked better, and we kept more of our money working for us right here. Unfortunately, offshoring became the new easy way of bumping profits, but with that came a decline in quality.

There was a time you'd take your TV in for repair! That's not happening much anymore, you just go down and buy a new one. Tools by Craftsman© were something that lasted; now, if you get one of their garden tools, you might just be getting another next year, or season. It's just a rental, not a purchase. Do they really wonder why Sears is going away? It's gone offshore.

Most chain stores won't carry USA products because they're competing with the other chain stores and American-Made products look very expensive next to the cheap knockoffs. And so, quality gets watered down, the spiral continues as the offshore producers chip away at the specifications, making ever lower quality the new standard.

China, Inc. is the leader of this process. Now, because some folk have started to pay attention to that, they may leave off the country of origin from some of their packaging. "Designed in the USA" doesn't help if it's cheapened in China. Predatory manufacturing practices and ignoring international patents are standard there.

Though it may seem ever more difficult to stay away from offshore products, long-term benefits will come to us if we pay attention. Voting with our pocketbooks can bring manufacturing back home. It's not easy to find American-Made. Sticker shock may also turn your head away, but quality pays its own reward. Purchasing a product, as opposed to renting it, will always prove a greater value.

If we all pay attention, we'll save a lot of dough in the long run and the short run. Manufacturers will pay attention; they do if you slap them in the face enough. Make an effort to vote with your pocketbook, we can bring jobs back if we really want it. Commitment to Excellence—let's make that our standard!

48. "Tell a lie loud enough and long enough and people will believe it." Adolph Hitler, thanks to azquotes.com on this

There are folk who stand behind Donald the First who will never gain a dime off his policies. The enormous contradictions of his policies evaporate in the minds of the staunch followers. The Great Self-Promoter has turned making up the facts as you go along, into a standard of his existence. P.T. Barnum, formerly the Greatest Self-Promoter of All Time, couldn't hold a candle to He Who Should Never Be Questioned.

There are many who blindly follow along, because deep in their hearts, they want what he says to be truth—don't bother with facts or stats which say otherwise. Others follow because they feel to do otherwise would dismember the Republican Party. Still others give support because they're just anarchists and see the GOP as a great way of promoting government mayhem and shutdown. All together it comes up as a frothy mob to counteract.

Common Folk, which many of the above are actually a part of, will never be given an equal chance by the Child Haters. Big Money and Big Business are the power brokers fueling what the Republican Party stands for. Power PACs are out there flooding the internet with plenty of conspiracy fodder which is lapped up by those who just want to believe it's true. Once again, don't bother with documentable facts.

There are any number of the old guard Republicans who are not enchanted with the direction the party has taken. There was once a day, when I was just a lad, legislation was put forward, the two sides hammered out some form of compromise and the business of the nation was carried out. After all, the width and breadth of America contains people of varied beliefs, and no one wants one side's belief shoved down their throat.

Unfortunately, the "No Taxes, No Government" group has taken on a religious zeal for its beliefs, resulting in their trying to shove their policies en masse, without recognizing they are not representing all the people. They don't want to hear any ideas which don't follow their simple beliefs. They would rather hold their ears and go, "Mine, mine, mine, mine, mine!"

Misinformation and misdirection have become their strength. They will now never answer questions directly but rather throw blame elsewhere, make up stories about the questioners, or point out something unrelated to the question, avoiding an answer one way or the other. Helping the country is not on their radar, only in consolidating their power.

For them it's come down to gerrymandering districts way out of proportion, removing voters from the rolls, and supporting the internet operatives which discourage those who would otherwise vote against them. Making people believe they're "stickin' it to the man" by not voting helps keep them in business.

The whole process is quite scary especially when you have some-one at the top who is all about "ME!" Having this megalomaniac in charge, who has the gift of believing he is the best at everything, wants to maintain power beyond term limits, and thinks whatever pops into his head is great because it popped into his head, leads one to find we have power brokers who want to move away from Democracy.

The consolidation of power and money has put us on a precipice which, with hope, will not push us into an era where the rich achieve ultimate control. We did have that revolution back in the late 1700s, which threw off the mantle of the noble class and gave people the right to vote. Once again, I'll say the system isn't perfect, but that is only because it is run by us inherently imperfect humans. There is one person out there who believes He Is Perfect.

He Who Believes In His Perfection has shown that He Believes In Only Himself. No one who has ever left his employ would consider him to be the perfect boss. Micromanagement and mega-belittlement are his greatest strengths. And yes, he keeps a fleet of buses to throw people under because he will never take responsibility. Always there will be everyone else to blame.

The string of failed businesses he has left behind attest to inabil-ity to see anything through. Given his way, he'll fail the US Govern-ment, too. Certainly, no domestic lender will give him personal cash. All he borrows now for his future failures comes from foreign sources. He looks with envy at what Putin, Erdogan, and Kim Jong-un have—ultimate control. It seems, now, he is controlled by what they represent.

We, the people, must endeavor to never allow this behavior to ever be rewarded again. We, the people, must exercise our right to vote. We, the people, must ensure that voting is undertaken fairly and verifiably. Be active. At least twice a year. Vote. It's not a burden, it's a right! For now. Let's keep it that way! Don't let the lies become acceptable. Let's not be bamboozled, again!

49. "I'm mad as hell, and I'm not going to take this anymore!" character Howard Beale in Network 1976

Phew, well, that's how I feel after reading what I just wrote. So, let's move on and consider real world ideas and moving forward to make things better for the vast majority of us. Trickle Up—An Idea Whose Time Has Come! Raising the minimum wage, providing early education, getting healthcare for all—including mental health, vision, medical, and dental—will go a long way toward making this a better country for all.

Those three things alone will relieve some of the greatest stresses people now endure. Few people will need assistance like food stamps. It will make us a smarter country. We'll need that to continue to be leaders in industry and innovation. It will make us a healthier country and that will reduce healthcare costs in the long run. Let's emphasize long run. We must consider long-term solutions which will carry us as a nation into a brighter future.

No griping about "who's going to pay for all of this!" We are already paying for it; it just is in a haphazard and inefficient way and the playing field is totally uneven. In leveling the playing field, everyone will benefit. Everyone. When the people on the other side of the tracks get equal treatment, everyone benefits. Education level will go up. Crime will go down.

If it's worth saying once, it's worth repeating; leveling the playing field will be a benefit for Everyone! They Who Don't Want to Pay for Anything will never understand inherent benefits of making sure everyone has access to a complete education from day one, a living wage, and medical care. Leveling the field will make us a far better country.

The religious like zeal of the Child Haters makes them rail against ideas they did not come up with. As noted, that means almost any idea, as they can only come up with "Borrow Money and Give It To The Wealthy." Any other idea is outside their conceptual capability. Socialism-For-The-Rich has proven only that money gets to concentrate farther up the food chain.

Currently, there is plenty of wealth in our nation; unfortunately, the bulk of it does not benefit us, the common people. Trickle Down is not a thing. It hasn't worked since its inception in the 1980s. You don't have to look far to see that ever since the concept started, wealth has further concentrated to fewer hands. It is time to try Trickle Up.

There are people out there that say the poor rich folk already pay a lot in taxes. Billionaires are not in danger of extinction. Overall taxation in the United States is lower than all the other developed countries. That has been established. Raising taxes on billionaires won't collapse the economy. Part of leveling the field of income inequality is letting those who can most readily afford it, pay. It's not as if they'll have to move into one of the tenements they may own.

Really, instituting Trickle Up will provide greater security for all Americans. Overall, the raising of the minimum wage will allow more people to live a better life. Affording better groceries will help people think better! Who doesn't get a bit cranky when they're hungry? Proper education, from early on, will lead to better decision making. Having healthcare for all will lead to healthier lives. Trickle Up! We can make this happen for the benefit of all.

50. Costs and Consequences

Everything we do comes with costs and consequences. It's better to pay for the costs right up front. For instance, plastic. It's everywhere. Unfortunately. It's covering a significant portion of the planet. Right up front, plastic manufacturers should be putting into the clean-up-of-the-planet jar. They'll moan, "Why us?" Of course, the answer is because this is where the problem begins.

The costs will be passed on to us, as, after all, we pay for everything. Putting it in at the start of the process makes it a smaller bite. We all know small bites are easier to swallow. The manufacturers already have accountants to handle this additional line item on their spreadsheets. They don't like line items, sure, but they can handle this one.

So, we take this money from the plastic jar, and it creates new jobs! Clearing the oceans of all that plastic can provide lots of good paying jobs. Plastic bags are the modern-day tumble weed. Let's clean that up, too. More jobs. Recycling plastic—more jobs! We don't need to send it back across the ocean to let some other country recycle it.

If we paid, say, a penny extra for every baggie to create these jobs, will it break our bank? Nope. If the tax is built into the product, spreading out costs, small bites will hardly be noticed. All plastic products should be taxed at the source to create jobs. It is fair and equitable. As a line item at the manufacturer, we won't see the small bite we're providing. We will be helping to clean up the massive mess we managed to create.

Cleaning up the ocean is in everyone's best interest. Some might say, "Hey! I don't eat fish. Why should I care?" The oceans are an integral part of the food chain we all share, whether you're dining on sea bass, barbeque ribs, or Impossible™ Burgers. Everyone is more dependent on the oceans than they know. The health of the ocean is essential to the health of the planet.

Another consequence we can pay for is carbon dioxide. Deniers will claim paying carbon taxes will be bad for business. Ninety-nine point nine percent of scientists say it will cost more if we don't start doing something right now. Who wants to build a twenty-foot higher seawall? No one. It could come to that. Carbon taxes to pay for planting trees and supporting clean energy projects will provide jobs! Again, many of these clean energy jobs should be brought to the coal belt, where jobs have been lost.

Five cents a gallon on gasoline and diesel is a small bite to go towards The Trillion Tree Initiative. Planet-wide, this would be a fabulous course of action. We have, as a species, been cutting down trees for thousands of years without replanting. We didn't understand what we were doing! Then, industrialization came along. We pushed the balance right over the edge!

It will take time to plant a trillion trees, but this is not an impossible task. There is plenty of land, especially in the higher elevations of the expanding Sahara, available for just this sort of thing and anyone can add to the total. With determination and tenacity, we can accomplish this, and, within fifty years, the difference will be seen and felt. Doing nothing accomplishes nothing. It may seem inefficient, but we should replace our ancient forest land. Eventually, when enough is planted, and the forests have emerged, the forests will draw the clouds and rain.

Planet-wide, because the world really needs to join in on this one, there are other issues which should be addressed. Those living subsistent lives need to be given a way to cook their meals without cutting down trees. Trees are being cut down to make coal out of rainforest. It may seem counter to cutting down carbon production, but providing small efficient fuel stoves and the fuel to run them will keep more trees upright and produce less carbon overall.

We need to work together on this as a planet, but we can start right here in the US.

Perhaps you have heard the story that there is more forest now in the US than there was in 1900. The correct way of presenting that would be to say there is more land in forest production now than there was in 1900. Previous to that, they just kept cutting down, for farmland, building or heating, replanting was not on the radar.

So now, yes, there may be more land in forest production, but that doesn't mean there is actually more forest. If you've ever flown over the forests of Oregon, say, you notice a checkerboard pattern of forest and clear-cut. Counting clear-cut as forest is cheating. That is not forest,

forest production maybe, but not forest. At least we are replanting the forest production land.

Let's take out these small bites to pay for the consequences of our actions. Industries won't crumble. Capitalism won't be compromised. The End Of Civilization As We Know It won't happen. More jobs will happen. Good, clean jobs! Well, planting trees may get a little dirty.

51. "Water, water everywhere, nor any drop to drink."
     From The Rime of the Ancient Mariner by Samuel
     Taylor Coleridge

Over 70 percent of the earth surface is water, only 3 percent is fresh. Water is the most important resource on the planet. Chocolate, especially dark, is also important, but water makes it all possible. Drinkable water is extremely important. Let's talk about it.

Climate change deniers can say all they want, but weather is becoming more unpredictable. There are large populations in desert areas, like LA or Phoenix, that have unsustainable water resources. The aquifers are drying up, and the land is sinking! We will all have to come to terms with this. What can we do about water?

Fortunately, we do have oceans of the stuff, all we need do is make it potable. Systems are in place in various locations around the globe to address that very thing, like the Mideast. Converting sea water into drinking water is certainly not as cheap as pulling it from an aquifer, stream, or lake. Coming up with more efficient systems to turn it into drinking water should become one of the next big things in research.

We currently have billionaires who are in a race to get to Mars! Very exciting stuff. It's a dry planet. Though, personally a big fan of space exploration, perhaps some of those billions of dollars could go into providing drinking water to billions of people. That would really be exciting. Universities should have programs devoted to the subject.

Producing water from the ocean will cost more, but it is a cost which can be…absorbed. Just as the doubling of gasoline prices was absorbed so can the cost of providing potable water. A commitment must be made to begin with. The increase in this case would be gradual, not jarring. Most people live near the coasts already. This is doable.

At some point a decision about providing water for crops and people will have to be made. Crops require far more water than people, but the crops must be watered, or we can't have people. We will pay for this somewhere along the line and no better time than when we can be ahead of the curve. Watering people uses a lot less water, and as a nation, we've already begun the process. How many bottles of water are sold each year?

When I was a lad, there were a mere three billion sharing the planet. Current estimates say there are now over seven billion. We are successfully producing people. They don't all have clean water taps. Bad water is the source of disease. Clean water for people is a great investment and a lot cheaper than healthcare!

Innovation for providing potable water is a fabulous cause. Solar distilleries? Sure. Let's tap into the cash resources and alleviate water shortages! C'mon, you billionaires, put a few drops into this research! Everyone needs water.

52.   "We might as well require someone to wear still the coat which fitted them when a child as civilized society to remain ever under the regimen of their barbarous ancestors." Thomas Jefferson, paraphrased to remove gender specifics…

This is for the elders who still believe that straddling in the middle will get the greatest votes. We who have lived longer into the current situation may like to think middling is best. In order to get the young generation on board, broadening our scope to bring them into the conversation and seeing with their eyes what we have wrought, we must now move into a new era where positive change will engage younger voters.

We must turn the tide by effecting policies which will benefit the greater good so we can leave the yellers and screamers behind while giving hope to the young that they, too, can achieve life, liberty, and the pursuit of happiness in their time. Today's young voter is disillusioned. Housing prices have risen astronomically, wages have been stagnant, healthcare costs continue to rise, and the escalation of hate and vitriol from the extreme conservatives leaves our new potential voters in a state of shock over what they have inherited.

The six main points brought up at the beginning of this pamphlet are the cornerstones of moving into a brighter future for all. In some form or another, these changes must be embraced and enacted. Boldly we must go, while the din of the Child Haters drones on with no plan or template to address the change needed, and we must show clearly that status quo can end. We have limped through the last forty years because it has suited Republicans to do nothing, because that doesn't cost them anything.

A new economy with living wages and healthcare. An economy which recognizes climate change needs addressing and provides jobs where they have been lost. An economy where retirees can rely on Social Security as a steady income. A place where their children can grow and thrive with education, and they can live in the home of their dreams.

There is no looking back. It's time to take that bold step forward and let our new adults know we have a democracy here which can effect change benefitting all. Removing the Citizens United decision where people and organizations with money can run roughshod over the internet and airwaves is paramount. Impugning the free press, Big Money wants to corral the voters into believing Big Business will eventually solve all our problems. They had their chance.

There is hope, because progressive change is achievable. Yes, it will cost money, but we are the richest country and can afford to get things done right. There is hope, because we can elect leaders who believe positive change can happen by throwing status quo out the window. No more plodding along. Step with courage knowing the jobs we will be creating will by their very nature create more jobs.

This is the vision we need to instill. We can make the American Dream spur our new generations to aspire to even greater heights. It is not a pipe dream; it is achievable with will and determination. We can make this happen. Let's give the new voters something to hold in front of them and say, "We can do this!" Rosie would agree.

53. Door Number 1, Door Number 2 or Door Number 3. Choosing Healthcare Is Not as Easy As 1, 2, 3

We have been trained for a long time to make choices of a multitude of insurance plans to find one that best meets our personal needs. It is always mind-boggling at best. The upshot of all those choices was that we are placed in a smaller group, which would water down our power as a group. If we, as a nation, are considered one group, our power is greatest. Any discussion of the future of healthcare must begin with that principal—we are a group of one.

Insurance companies naturally want to divide up that power. This just diminishes all the plans and makes for greater inequity. Charging more because you are overweight, old, have previous issues like diabetes or congenital disabilities, are going to have a baby, or excluding you for these or any other reasons makes equitable healthcare impossible. We are one group and must move forward as one.

Eliminating profit at the expense of our health will save billions of dollars. Having our healthcare outcomes decided by those want to pad their stock options will never make for better results. Yes, there will be those claiming this will lead us down the path of Socialism, Communist takeover, and the end of civilization as we know it. What it will do is lead us down the path of affordable, more responsive healthcare.

Many people are fearful that a lack of choice may prevent them from getting the plan they want. Having had to make choices over all these years has some folks worried about not having a choice. If we start with a plan that includes everyone and all the best from any plan, the choice will be simple. Having the choice of what our representatives in Congress get is just a start. The finish line is not having people go broke to pay for their healthcare.

Recently, in Nevada, a unionized group agreed to a health plan which they don't want to see get ruined by Medicare-for-All. Let's start with that and make it better. The rest of the industrialized world has National Healthcare. The US is the last holdout for making universal healthcare a right. Healthcare should be a right. There should never be a reason for denial of healthcare. If you're laid off and between jobs, that shouldn't make it more expensive for you.

Paying for National Healthcare is a problem only if you focus on "What's it going to cost?" To reiterate, we are already paying for healthcare. Let that sink in for a minute. Healthcare is already being paid for, by and large. Where we go from here is just getting it to everyone, without having to sluff off billions to pay an unnecessary middleperson to siphon off funds that would otherwise go to actual healthcare. National Healthcare will save money, not cost us more.

National Healthcare will cost less than the system we have now. Fear of change makes us wonder, "How will this new system ever work?" It will work with greater efficiency. We already pay for our healthcare. It's time we took control as a group of one to make it work for everyone. Dissenters to this are the ones who won't get their cut of the pie. They can find another pie.

We already pay for healthcare. Currently, reinventing the infrastructure of paying for it doesn't have to happen. We are already paying it. We're already paying for those who don't have it, too. One way or the other, it's already being paid for. Making a group of one will just make it more efficient and equitable. Using small bites to cover the differences will make it easier to transition.

Not having to worry about paying for healthcare or where you're going to get it will end a lot of stress in everyone's life. That, in itself, will improve our health! Don't worry about the number of choices. Let's just have the best. That's the simple choice. We have the technology, the knowledge, the skills, and the ultimate ability to deliver the best. There is no reason to settle for less than that!

54. Billionaires Are Not in Danger of Extinction

Raising the minimum wage to a living wage will make life better for everyone, even the billionaires. More people with more money will bump the economy. The billionaires will surely benefit. Supply Siders will shake their heads; it's what they do. They don't want to mention that, since the 1970s, CEO pay and executive pay has outpaced line worker pay across the board by ten to one hundred times. Another example of wage inequity.

Moving towards a fifteen-dollar-an-hour minimum will begin an end to wage inequity. It's all about the new trickle up policy we need to implement to get us where everyone will have a chance to succeed. Recognizing the value of everyone's contribution is important for getting us to the point where inequity isn't built into the system.

If our Aussie friends can support what is currently about twenty dollars per hour, we can surely start at fifteen dollars, and it just has to be a start. Indexing it with inflation year after year is essential. Currently, the National Minimum Wage hasn't changed for ten years. That is unconscionable. The minimum should always be indexed, without the whims of Congress to impede it.

Part of a living wage is affordable housing. In Seattle, home prices have skyrocketed in the last twenty-five years. Wages have not. Seattle isn't the only area where housing costs have gone up, and we're not the most expensive. The disparity between rising housing costs and wages has kept a lot of people from achieving the dream of home ownership. We must reawaken that dream.

Raising the tide means bringing the minimum up to a living wage. Small businesses will flinch at the prospect, and there will be a transition while everyone gets used to paying a little more for certain things. Coupled with National Healthcare, small businesses will be better able to compete with Big Business to retain quality employees who might otherwise leave for better benefits elsewhere. The small businesses will find that more people will be able to afford their wares.

There will be a transition, but if we take a breath, let it take hold, and run with it—all will benefit in the long haul. We can make this work. It's been proven to work Down Under. Many countries already do it. Big Business will survive, billionaires will continue to proliferate, and greater job satisfaction will follow. Let's emphasize job satisfaction because a living wage will bring that.

55.   We Pay for Everything—All Jobs are Paid for By Us

Make no mistake about it. Any job you see or do is being paid for by all of us. We, as a group, pay for these jobs by our daily purchases, taxes, and donations. Where you spend your money creates jobs. All jobs come out of our collective pocketbook. Please consider this as you go about doling out your paycheck.

Where do you want to see your money go? Everything we buy makes an investment in that company, country, or industry. If you want better infrastructure, we will have to pay for it. We have to pay for everything. Every time I use my credit card, I think, "I'm priming the economy." We prime the economy every time we spend our hard-earned dollars. Wouldn't you rather see your money stay here in the US?

That would be ideal but, currently, very difficult. It shouldn't be so hard. Paying for living wages typically costs more than supporting oversea economies. Seeing the value in spending more for a product can be a hard sell when the difference in cost seems so great; however, if you factor in quality and longevity, long-term costs may be the same or less.

Small items made of stainless steel are particularly troublesome. Right out of the package, these small items have tended to be mere ghosts of the products which were available even ten years ago. Dissatisfaction with a new product has become routine. Made in China seems like a trademark for "short term rental." I'd rather pay twenty dollars for something Made in America, whose quality is top notch, than pay $2.99 for something that might not be satisfactory for three months. It's a waste of material, money, and time.

Currently, it's difficult to track down quality American-Made goods. It's time we encouraged producers to bring us well-made stainless-steel goods. It would be easier if we were given the option, but the typical department store only sells the usual array of cheaply made products all the other stores carry. We'll be the third world economy if we can't get back to making simple products with quality and integrity in mind.

Integrity is essential. Ignoring ecological standards is standard in China. The air quality in their big cities is a testament to that. Run-off into rivers? They'll say it's because they are a growing economy, and they can't compete otherwise. That doesn't make them competitive, just careless. We have ecological standards in this country to protect our health. We shouldn't pay for another country's carelessness, especially if it's the next biggest economy.

Conservatives here want to roll back regulations which were made to ensure the quality of our health and neighborhoods. Those regulations are there not only to safeguard our health, it's to safeguard our land. Those regulations create jobs we need to keep us heathier; they are not job killers. Yes, it shows up in Big Business on their line items which they hate to see, but we're paying for it, one way or another, and at our end, it's not even pennies on the dollar.

The difference in cost to us is negligible in regard to most regulations—it's the line items on the Big Business ledger that sticks in their craw. Getting things done right costs more. We should want things to be done right. The cost to us at the far end is relatively low per job we pay for. Wait, do I hear someone railing about regulation? Our health and the health of the environment are directly related. Please, look up the statistics on cancer rates in the coal industry and in the areas surrounding coal mines. Would you rather pay for cancer treatments or prevention of harmful chemicals getting into the soil and air? To paraphrase the Declaration of Independence—We hold these truths to be self-evident.

Cost and consequence are a recurring theme if you've been reading. Paying for things done right will always pencil out. Making things that will last longer is always more cost efficient. Doing things that benefit the environment is cheaper than repairing the damage to health and land later. It always is cheaper and less painful to pay these costs upfront.

Make a statement with your wallet. Choose to spend from it to put your Fellow Americans to work, whenever you can. It's a choice that will also benefit you in the long run. The more people working good jobs here will keep our neighborhoods safer from crime and more jobs will be created from those jobs. This is a win-win situation.

We all contribute to the jobs we work. It is a known aspect of job creation in any industry, that jobs outside that industry get created to support it. That's the way it always works. Job creation generates more job creation. There really is plenty of work that needs to get done. Infrastructure is crying for attention. Roads, water, and energy generation all need to get brought up to date. There is no time like the present to get these projects underway. Let's pay for more jobs.

56. "Don't Fire Until You See the Whites of Their Eyes!"
Quote attributed to Col. William Prescott at the
Battle of Bunker Hill

This was one of the most astute commands ever given. When you're low on ammunition to begin with and are using firearms of questionable accuracy, it's best to maximize each shot. It also takes a bit of resolve when you've already been fired on, and a great deal of bravery. Reloading didn't come easy, either. Such were the tools of war back when the country was young.

This brings me to the matter of the much-debated Second Amendment. Back in the day, folks were funneling in the gunpowder, dropping in the shot, and then come up firing. If you weren't in the middle of a fire fight, you had a moment to consider about firing again. These were the weapons available when they said the right to keep and bear arms shall not be infringed.

Once again, I'd like to point out TJ's (Thomas Jefferson) mention of barbarous ancestors. He was talking about himself and his current collection of statespeople. They couldn't have foreseen what would become of available firearms. As a firm believer in the right, it's also important to take into consideration what we have wrought in the meantime.

The industry likes to bring up that guns don't kill, people do. If we had real National Healthcare with a strong mental health division, we could possibly cut down on the rampages we continue to witness. Let's consider if the Framers of the Constitution would have felt assault rifles, bazookas, or hand-held rocket launchers should be available in their neighbor's arsenal. That's quite a long way from stuffing powder down the barrel and following that up with the next pellet.

Reasonable people don't think background checks to be so great an infringement. It's harder to get a driver's license than it is to purchase a gun. Sure, driving isn't guaranteed in the Constitution, and it also leads to a lot of deaths. Coming up with solutions to cut down the deaths is what this is all about.

The industry would have to worry that a database of registered gun owners would eventually be used against the gun owners. Don't worry, Big Brother (or Sister) is already here! Hi, Alexa! Hi, Siri! Databases are filling up all the time! The Eyes are upon us, and we take them with us.

The background system as it currently stands is haphazard at best. States have one or more agencies handling guns, and the FBI's database is inadequate, sadly, for getting the job done with accuracy and completeness. Closing up the loopholes for acquiring guns, like background checks at trade shows, would go a long way toward assuring the safety of the greater population.

57. "…speak softly and carry a big stick…" Theodore Roosevelt's Basic Foreign Policy

When the twentieth century was young, these were fresh words. Now, in the twenty-first century, yelling and incapacity to listen are the watch words of the day. Fake news is primed by those who are willing to shout out their opinions and pass them on as truths. Listening is a long-lost art.

Expressing your feelings has led to shouting down the opposition. Civil discourse has gone the way of the dodo. Why can't we be friends? The Child Hating Conservative wants their way or the highway. Compromise impedes their passion. Compromise eliminates their Right. "No Taxes, No Government," borrowing money for the rich, this is their Commitment. Unwaveringly.

They of the Bad Math Camp can't listen to other's ideas. It impugns their religious belief that starving government is the only way to salvation. Instead of engaging in conversation about improving the lives of us common folk, they'd rather call people names like, Communist! Socialist! Or say, "Regulation strangles business!"

Engage to listen, listen to engage. Once upon a time, even back in the '60s and '70s, compromises were worked out, and the business of government was attended to without threatening shutdowns or other grandstanding. Yes, there were yellers back then and before, but differences were worked out. Finger pointing and name calling weren't standard procedure.

It will take work to get us back to civil discourse in politics. It starts with voting in representatives who will legislate for the common folk. Using the vote to get true representation. Vote out those who think Big Business will solve our problems; it won't. Vote in people who believe in government, that it can be used for positive change in our daily lives.

Let's vote in representatives who discuss things rationally, respecting that it's okay to have a difference of opinion but consider the import of what's being said. Of course, common sense is in the eye of the beholder. Sensibility with compassion and understanding makes for a well-rounded opinion.

Bad math has to be removed from the table. Borrowing from our offspring leads to imbalance. A lot more could be accomplished if we weren't spending over three hundred billion dollars a year just to service our debt. There is no justification for continuing a policy of borrowing money when the economy has been doing as well as it has been for almost ten years, now. Balancing the budget makes sense, though, it might require Uncommon Sense.

Paying down the debt should be a priority. So much more could be accomplished if this debt wasn't there. It will take work to put the people in place who have a grasp of fiscal responsibility. It will take a lot of votes. I have faith that more folks now understand that exercising their right to vote is imperative, especially since there are those who are actively trying to take that right away.

Listening, taking Big Money out of the process, and balancing a complex budget are qualities we need in our elected leaders. Believing we can borrow our way to prosperity has got to stop. Being proactive in politics for us common folk means only having to get out to vote twice a year. That's all it takes. Let's all be proactive and elect leaders with good math skills.

The yellers and finger-pointers need to be cast aside. We all have them in our families and places of work. Shouters making sure you don't get heard. Repeating the same thing over and over again because that makes them right. That is not the Right we need. It's time to turn the other way. Listen to the hopes and dreams of the 99 percenters. We deserve to have our time in the sun. Let's vote to let the 99 percent get heard!

58.   Wage Security, Not War

As already stated, the contingent who voted to borrow more money to give to the well-to-do and large corporations, hate their children and their children's children. They have chosen to drop their fiscal irresponsibility into the laps of future generations. Reagan began this religion, referring to it as Trickle Down. They got the trickle part right.

Ordinary people will never benefit from this. As a group, we must vote to bring fiscal sense to the table. We can raise the tide for the benefit of all. Funnel Up has only concentrated the money—and power—into fewer and fewer hands. It's in the record for anyone to see. Trickle Up can be the way to move toward inverting income inequality.

We must be firm and unwavering. Voting every time. Making sure our friends and family vote. Speak firmly into the howling of the foot-stomping Bad Math Party. They have fooled some people for all time, let's not let them take the rest of us along on that ride again. It has already been proven Trickle Down works only for the 1 percent.

Let's listen to the needs of ordinary folk, the small business, the small farm, we who actually get the work done that keeps our nation rolling. Big Business doesn't need another Congressional Act to help it out; it's already BIG. They throw around the big employment numbers and make it sound so enticing. Let's think small!

Small business needs the help! Small farms need help! The common worker needs a living wage to support their neighborhood business and farmer's market. Thinking small is the next Big Thing! Let's rally our thinking towards the Trickle Up movement. Everyone will benefit, everyone, even the Big Boys, though they won't see it that way.

Getting the hardcore Child Haters on board won't be easy. It may not be possible, but it's worth a try. Benefitting everyone, well, that benefits everyone. It's a great thought. A living wage is the start. More people with more money will help the economy. It will Trickle Up. Even billionaires will get the benefits!

Listen to the simple sense of that. Putting more money into more people's hands will expand the economy. It will create a synergy like the loaves and fishes. It stimulates the imagination. Imagine home ownership being within the grasp of a greater portion of the population. That really would be something.

We can make this happen. I saw it in Australia. If they can do it there, we certainly can get it done here. Raising the minimum wage can staunch the Cycle of Poverty. There are the Big Businesses out there who don't want their supply of Cheap Labor to go away. Let's put Serfdom behind us. Let's think Big, for us common folk. We may be wage slaves, but we needn't work for slave wages.

Ending the Cycle of Poverty starts with a living wage. Raising the tide creates a boon for all. Skeptics will abound, and there will be those who will say it will stymie job creation. If it's a job that needs to get done, it should be paid out in living wages.All jobs that need to be done should be respected by a living wage.The economy will adjust. It always does.

The majority of jobs won't be affected by a raise in the minimum wage; they are already being paid out at more than that. Bringing up the floor of the scale is the only way to correct income inequality.Adjusting to it won't take long, because it will benefit everyone.As the benefits are realized, adjustment to the greater minimum will be easier to accept.

It has been ten years since the minimum was raised; that is what is called deferred maintenance. Deferred maintenance is the Republican Standard.That is why being aggressive by stepping up pay isn't a leap to fifteen dollars an hour, just catching up with inflation.Tying it to the Consumer Price Index is essential. You may wonder why it wasn't already? Darn good question, glad you brought that up!

A living minimum wage should always be raised by the annual Consumer Price Index.That is the way it should always have been.Take out the need for yearly Congressional action to keep wages competitive with living. Keeping up with the rent shouldn't mean working two or three jobs just to stay afloat.

Many parts of the country had housing costs skyrocketing until the Bush Recession arrived, crashing the real estate markets which had been driving the economy. Suddenly, jobs were lost, and because mortgages were more than the value of the property, people started losing their homes. Despite the job numbers being touted currently, there are still many folks out there that never recovered from 2008.

Homelessness increased rapidly at that time, and all you have to do is look around to see it has only gotten worse. Rent in Seattle is not cheap. (Please insert the name of any number of other cities.) If you want the people who provide essential services to be able to live in the communities they work, we'll have to raise their pay.

It can be daunting, legislating a leap to a living wage, scary to some. The economy will adjust; it always does. We survived the doubling (and more!) of energy costs in the 1970s during the "Energy Crisis." OPEC had summarily raised prices. We panicked, but survived. Energy affected the cost of just about everything. We coped and moved on. A Living Wage won't involve all aspects of the economy.

Jumping up the minimum wage will bring security and hope to millions. The spread-out cost to everyone will be pennies on the dollar. More people will have more money to spend. The economy benefits. It's time to raise the tide, turn the tables, and Funnel Up! Let's make this the beginning of the end of Poverty! We can afford it!

59. Better Healthcare Leads to Better Health

Who knew?! A study based on letters sent out by the IRS discovered this to be true. In 2016 the IRS sent out letters to 3.9 million who had been fined for not carrying health insurance but included ways to sign up. Due to budget constraints, six hundred thousand did not receive the letter. Three Treasury Department economists found that the notices got more people to sign up, and for those that did, one fewer death occurred per 1,648 for those who received a letter than those than those who hadn't, saving about seven hundred lives!

Imagine the possibilities if everyone had health insurance. Certain naysayers for true National Healthcare say that even uninsured get emergency care, as ERs are required to treat all patients regardless of their ability to pay. Two things on this: Everyone pays for this because it comes out of the hospital's general budget, which is paid for one way or the other, by us. The second thing: Emergency care is more expensive. If the uninsured could have gone to the doctor before, emergency care wouldn't have been needed.

We paid for that. It may be redundant to remind us once again that, one way or another, we are currently paying for all healthcare in the United States. The lack of a cohesive plan for everyone makes the delivery of health services more costly and inefficient. The tens of thousands of health plans out there chop up services haphazardly to small groups that the insurance companies just use to benefit shareholders and line the pockets of the boardroom execs.

Taking our National Healthcare out of private insurance will put more of the dollars spent on healthcare into actual healthcare. It will also take our healthcare decisions out of the boardroom and into the hands of the doctors and nurses who are giving the care. We don't need thousands of always confusing choices in insurance plans to make healthcare work for us. One plan that covers everybody will do, and it will do it at less cost.

Socialism! Communism! Dogs and cats living together! Putting some name tag on taking medical care out of the hands of those extracting unnecessary sums from the middle of medical costs doesn't make a rational argument on how to better the delivery of healthcare. The Child Haters don't get they're already paying for this but aren't getting the best bang for their buck. Call National Healthcare by this name—efficiently delivered healthcare.

In the long run, covering everyone will result in better overall health. Overall costs will go down. If people get a chance to see a doctor when the problem is small, emergency care won't be the first resort when a problem gets bigger. Look at that first paragraph about seven hundred lives saved out of a small sample. Let's save more lives! That would be something!

As Americans, we have been given choices and been able to choose amongst them. It's the American Way. Simplifying the medical care choice can seem new, scary, and a depravation of making a choice. What is so hard about just getting the best? Choosing the best seems simple enough. Something that covers whatever ails you. You'll still be able to pay extra for specialty clinics to lift your eyebrows, tuck your tummies and chins, but that'll be on your dime. True healthcare should be covered.

It's being paid for already. We just need to make it more efficient. Just taking the middle person out of the equation may be enough to cover everyone. Making a single payor system gives us true National Healthcare. Moving toward single payor will make delivering healthcare more efficient. Medicare-For-All isn't enough. A story in the August 8th, 2019 Lynden (WA) Tribune relates how a couple in their '70s killed themselves because they couldn't afford their healthcare. Medicare doesn't go far enough.

Pulling it all together will take work, mostly due to the people kicking and screaming who will hang onto the current outdated and inefficient system because that is what they know. It might be like pulling teeth, getting certain folk to wrap their heads around what is a perfectly sensible approach. The math says better access to healthcare leads to better health. Better health will lead to less money spent on healthcare.

To some, it's a dizzying concept. Granted, we will begin something new and different than what we are used to. Just because it's different doesn't mean it has to be complicated. Simple is best, the best is the simple solution. Medicare-For-All isn't simple. Have you ever spoken with someone on Medicare and their dizzying array of options and plans? We can do better.

Choosing between healthcare plans is stressful. Discovering the hole in your option is stressful. Eliminating the stress of options by providing complete all-around healthcare will contribute to better health in itself – less stress! Once everyone is on board, receiving complete healthcare, the obvious benefits will start to show through and manifest themselves as time goes by.

Cheers! To Everyone's Good Health!

60. Science, Technology, Engineering, and Math

Education is the only way to stay ahead in an ever-advancing world of technology…and misinformation. STEM disciplines are not for everyone, but they must be emphasized. We can only hold onto our current state of economic leadership by continuing research and development of advancing technology by our own engineers. Thousands of H-1B visas are issued every year to borrow hi-tech engineers from out of the country. We need to produce more right here. The hi-tech industry is pulling down a lot of dough, maybe they can send some of it back to beef up the STEM programs at our colleges and universities.

Local colleges in Seattle and the state of Washington are hard pressed to expand engineering programs. State funding for higher education waned over the years and is only now starting to catch up. Competition for students to get into engineering has made many students chose other programs. We are failing our brightest by not having enough room for them to get the training they need to help us compete in this highly competitive world.

As a nation, we can't afford to fall behind. It is an imperative for us to provide ample space in engineering programs so all our best students can succeed at what will keep our country competitive far into the future. Underfunding our universities will always hold us back.

For every H-1B visa, there is someone already here that wanted that job but couldn't get it because there wasn't room in our universities to give them the proper education. We are shortchanging ourselves on this one, and it also allows more of the technology we design to end up moving out of the country without compensation.

STEM may not be for everyone, but everyone interested in it should be given the chance to succeed. To lead in research and technological development, we need to support our institutions of higher learning. Success comes from providing access to every one of our own who is capable to do the work. Instead of begging for more H-1B workers from overseas, our Hi-Tech companies should be supporting our colleges to expand engineering programs.

61. Impeachment Demonstrates Separation of Powers

Impeachment is Congress's right to wield their power as an equal branch of government. It is a right, but it's a solemn exercise which should be used when the fabric of responsible government is being threatened. Impeachment was voted on by the House of Representatives, yesterday. It is a time when representative government is being extremely tested.

As the Executive Branch demeans the country's Armed Forces, Congress, and vital institutions with lies, deceit, and obstruction, all but declaring himself to be the Ultimate Power of the Nation, it becomes necessary to rein in these delusions of grandeur. Impeachment isn't a whim for Congress to indulge themselves in but a responsibility to ensure the stability of the Nation. The Donald has stretched the limits of the Executive Office in every way, saying he is Entitled and needn't cater to any other governmental agency.

By saying legitimate journalists only make fake news, he attempts to destroy a free press, even going so far as to say he'd like to start a "government-run" news agency. Putin is his idol in this regard. A free press is written into the Constitution. That's not to say fake news isn't being produced, because there is an unprecedented proliferation of fake news available on the internet. Impugning legitimate news sources degrades us all.

The amount of hate and vitriol Trump and his supporters spew can only be likened to the totalitarian regimes that want to wipe out discussion and dissent. That not one Republican Rep was willing to disapprove of his actions shows that they approve of his talk of never leaving office. It is frightening that they have all moved in the direction of wanting total control of the government, without room for ideas beyond their narrow beliefs.

As is usual when voicing their dissatisfaction with Impeachment, the Republicans speak only to process or partisanship, never to any of the offered facts which required Congress to take action. Our Constitutional Government is imperiled by He Who Would Be Emperor and the Conservatives who don't want to ever have to relinquish their power.

It is a power grab, and they have anointed Trump to be the leader to take them down this promised land of complete control. He has no boundaries. He is the leader they can count on to put himself above all else. This is the State of the Nation to which we have come to.

You can't say the Republicans in office lack the testicles to openly defy him; what they lack is integrity. If a Democrat had done all the same things, the torches and pitchforks would have been gathered, but for this Anointed One, they yield to their Majesty. The United States of America in now compromised.

These Conservatives will say the House of Representatives is trying to overturn the last election. What they won't mention is that their guy didn't get a majority of the vote, originally. Would that really be overturning the election then? It is the responsibility of Congress to use their right to keep checks and balances in place. It is an exercise in keeping the integrity of government in place. No one is above the law, especially the president. The president must be accountable to Congress and to the people.

These are very trying times; no one wants to put our nation through this wringer. It has come to this, though. Accountability in all our elected offices and those not elected makes for a truly strong nation. Let's let our strength and integrity show. Checks and balances will keep Democracy alive.

62. The Lowest Common Denominator

It is said that a group can't rise above its lowest common denominator. Education is the great equalizer. To remain at the forefront of innovation and in economic leadership, education must be provided to all. The earlier in life education is brought to our children, the greater the benefit will be to us as a nation.

Unfortunately, income inequality has struck at the very heart of providing the highest quality of education. Here in Seattle, a high school teacher with thirty-five years of experience and a master's degree makes ten thousand dollars less than a graduate fresh out of college going to code for a centralized business server conglomerate. If we want to retain quality teachers, we have to start by giving them high quality pay.

If you know any teachers, you will have heard stories of promising young people starting out in the profession but leaving after a year or two, due to the stress and lack of equitable pay. In Seattle, you need a lot of compensation to hope to be able to buy a home. A young teacher's pay wouldn't give you that light at the end of the tunnel.

Education is the most important thing we can give to children. It is the most important thing to keep us ahead in a very demanding and changing world. To keep excellent educators, we need to give them quality pay. The disparity between pay scales in the tech industries and what our essential teaching staffs receive is appalling.

Forking out the extra dough to pay for a good education will pay greater dividends down the road. We need to buck up to be able to provide the best possible schools. Cutting corners on education funding does not help us to succeed.

The profession of providing education needs elevation in the rank of importance to society. Educators should be up there with doctors, nurses, and firefighters, esteemed as essential to keeping us healthy and safe in an increasingly hostile world. Let's give them their due. As we raise them, we raise ourselves! Education is a priority. Proper compensation will lead to better retention of quality candidates. Our education staff deserves quality pay. Recognizing their true value is essential for keeping us at the vanguard of innovation and economic leadership.

63.   Making the Best Healthcare Choice

For so many years we have been inundated with a confusing array of healthcare insurance options. It's no wonder some people worry about Single Payor. Not having choices seems un-American! What if we didn't have to decide which is best because the plan is to provide the best quality care, without having to throw in the interests of shareholders or CEOs?

Starting with the healthcare options now available to our representatives in Congress, we can probably whittle down the decision-making process. As Americans, we do want to have the best available to us. As Americans, we are in great position to go ahead and provide what would be the best healthcare program on the planet. We already have doctors, hospitals, clinics, and emergency rooms available. The simple solution is: you decide which one you go to.

That would be the most American Way for healthcare to be addressed. The one plan system means you get to choose your provider; it's not chosen for you. What could be more American than getting to make your own choices? One health plan with over three hundred million subscribers would get the proper attention of drug manufacturers and medical providers in helping to keep costs down.

It is important to remember we especially want to keep our hospitals in business. In my nearly thirty years working for a medical system, it was curious how Medicare/Medicaid reimbursements for specific procedures would go down over the years. Hospitals would have to make up for that somewhere along the line, or refuse Medicare patients. It is imperative we keep our hospitals funded and especially able to cope with disasters like hurricanes, earthquakes, pandemics, and other natural and man-made disasters. Medicare and Medicaid patients are currently limited on their provider choices.

Individual choice for where to receive medical care should be up to the individual. That is an obvious choice. We shouldn't have to look through the fine print to see if diabetes, maternal care, dialysis, mental health, or contraception are on the list. Everything short of elective vanity procedures should be allowed so we can all live normal healthy lives. Looking through complex charts to see what the best compromise in delivering your healthcare to you should just not be necessary.

Providing all available health options to everyone's list makes for an equitable system. We can all live with that. We can all live better if everyone has access to good healthcare. Winding up in an emergency room because you couldn't pay to see the doctor when a problem was small should never occur again.

Making healthcare choices should be simple. The simplest choice is to have one Single Payor Plan which covers all of our choices. Complicating health plan choices with an A, B, C, or D auxiliary plan shouldn't be necessary. One plan, covering everyone, will make for the most efficient choice of them all. Let's have the best for everyone!

64. Getting Big Money Out of Politics

The Seattle Times headline from Wednesday, October 16, 2019, "Amazon spending $1.45 million on Seattle City Council Races." The concentration of money allows corporate spenders and the ultra-rich to exert undue influence on the outcomes of our elections. This has got to stop. The Citizens United decision rendered by an obviously influenced conservative Supreme Court must be reversed in Congress. We can never hope to have fair elections as long as Big Money can continue to dole out as much as they want to impact elections.

For the court to have conceived that free speech rights need to be given to corporate entities is ludicrous, at best. Once again, the poor rich folk have been given their "just due" by conservative ideologues who apparently believe Big Business should run the government.

The same conservative conscience says government should be run more like a business, yet they borrow money to hand out to the upper echelons of business and society. Do businesses in real life borrow money to hand out to their top executives and shareholders? No. The conservatives are running the government like an ATM for the rich.

We must reverse this attack on government by the people and for the people before government by the monied interests becomes entrenched. We are at a precipitous point in time where our vote needs to get out to take back government by the people. Everyone needs to get out to vote. We must let it be known we want a government representative of the common citizen, not the Big Monopolies.

If you want representative government, you must vote. You don't have a right to complain about the state of affairs if you haven't voted. Some of you out there have already had your right to vote compromised. Make sure you have a current registration, then get out and vote. Voting twice a year is not a hardship; it is a duty to your country, and yourself. Make no excuses. Be late for work or leave early. Better yet, get your state to join the many with mail-only ballots you can send in early if you like.

Government's primary purpose is to take care of the interests of its people, not the interests of Big Business. Currently, we are the richest country in the world; we should be paying our bills, not borrowing money to give to those who already have it. Government can be run like a business that pays its bills. There is no excuse for piling up more common debt, none.

The Citizens United decision can now only be overturned by legislation. That can only happen if we turn out to vote for people who will vote for people. People who make up the great majority of the population, the 99 percent. We've had forty years of trickle down which has shown itself to be funnel up. Money has been concentrating into fewer and fewer hands, both corporate and personal. It's time to right the ship, by turning left, of course.

Sure, the Bad Math contingent will spit out labels of Socialism!

Communists! Nanny State! It's easier to yell names than to discuss the actual issues: income inequality, healthcare, education, loss of competition in business through mergers and conglomeration. They can't talk about it, it tilts their brains, making them repeat: Socialism! Communism! Nanny State! Rational discourse is out of the question.

Let's vote in representatives who will turn away the tidal wave of entrenched money. The conservatives always speak of reducing entitlements but don't seem to see their efforts only make the Rich feel more entitled. Socialism for the Rich is their modus operandi. What if all the money Big Business spent on political advertisement went to jobs in infrastructure? That would be useful.

Let's get big money out of politics by voting in those who will legislate Citizens (horrific oxymoron) United out of existence. It should be on every candidate to do list, front and center. It should be on every citizen to do list. Madison Avenue might lose a lot of business, but it won't bankrupt them. We, the people, will survive.

65. Addressing Pay Inequity

Unfortunately, until the human race has rid itself of hidden and overt bias, there will always be inequity. Inherent bias can't be eliminated through legislation, but a living wage—providing security, a sense of self-esteem and pride in work can be legislated.

There will always be high-stress jobs, like doctors, nurses, and teachers, who by the nature of their work should be paid well. We want doctors, nurses, and other healthcare workers to want to continue in their jobs. If you don't pay enough for that kind of stress, who's going to want those jobs?

All jobs should provide a minimum wage that encourages showing up for work and a sense of completing tasks with pride. Everyone deserves that. If it's a job that needs to be done, it should come with compensation to live in decent housing and to eat healthy food. We are not serfs, working for a fiefdom; we threw off that aristocracy over two hundred years ago.

Fifteen dollars an hour as the national minimum will start putting us on a path for equity in pay across the board. Raising the tide to provide a living wage will raise the tide for all. Indexing the minimum wage yearly to the cost of living will ensure it doesn't lag behind the economy and workers can hope for greater security in their personal lives.

Income inequality for women, people of color, ethnicity, religion, or sexual identity must also end. Discrimination in any form divides us and benefits no one. We are all in this thing called life, together. We do all need each other to do all the various jobs required to make civilization work. Accepting individuals for who they are, without bias, will lead to greater income equality. No one should have to feel they are less deserving of equal treatment or that they can't get equal treatment.

Let's get on the bandwagon of making all jobs living wage jobs. When we raise the tide, the economy will benefit. There will be more people able to afford more things. It's the only way to work towards pay equality. We can't expect other folks to take a pay cut, except maybe a few billionaires. They'll muddle through.

66. "How We Gonna Pay for All This?"

As a reminder, when it comes to the national bill for healthcare, we are already paying for it. Not everyone has proper coverage, but we are all already paying these bills. When the uncovered go to the emergency rooms and their bill is written off? We pay for those bills, too. Not directly, but we are paying, one way or the other.

Critics of National Healthcare just like to point out the phenomenal cost of it all, looking at the big number it comes to. But wait, we are already paying that out! Critics of National Healthcare don't like to point out that the bill we are already paying is 20 percent higher than the next closest country. Are we getting 20 percent more? Not even close. National Healthcare will save us money! Don't be fooled by the naysayers throwing big numbers around, National Healthcare will cost less!

In the last twenty years our average life expectancy has gone down while everywhere else it keeps going up. The general health has eroded over this past twenty years. What is it about healthcare delivery in the US that has us sucking air on the "competition?" Could it be that the thousands of insurance plans out there we have available are taking cash out of actual healthcare delivery? The easy answer is, yes.

Another easy answer would be to cut this middle person out of the equation. The savings on this alone might be an easy 20 percent! Let's not quibble over that number, but just bear in mind there would be considerable savings. It would also save us from having our health-care decisions made by insurance companies. Let's save that dough and just put it all into healthcare.

Another piece of low hanging fruit to pick off would be lowering drug costs. Drugs are cheaper in every other country; why should we have to pay more? The drug manufacturers have an army of lobbyists out there who have managed to keep their companies from having to give up key patents, for one. How much cheaper would the drugs be if the manufacturers weren't paying for all these lobbyists?

If you have the imagination of Han Solo, it would be a lot of money. It doesn't take a lot of imagination to know we're getting the short end of the bargain. Anyone need an Epi-pen? What excuse can there be in raising the price six times? None worth listening to, but the sole man-ufacturer decided it had a monopoly that allowed it to charge whatever they wanted, the public be damned.

Sure, research and development costs need to be recovered, but beyond that, we don't need to prop up the penal profiteering practices of any company. If they're not making enough money selling pain re-lievers and cold medicines to keep the cash flow moving, we shouldn't have to suffer.

So, we can save a lot of money cutting out the middle person and showing up as a group of over three hundred million to negotiate sen-sible drug pricing. That in itself will save a flotilla of dough over time. Let's let medical professionals determine the course of healthcare. Yes, the Critics will want to just throw out the big number of overall cost National Healthcare solutions run, but discussing the benefits will never be in their wheelhouse. They will always just look at it as, Socialism! Nanny State! The end of Socialism for the Rich! Did they say that?

Let's get over the Big Cost of National Healthcare by just looking at the price tag. We are already paying it, just not as efficiently as we should. If everyone could go to the doctor when they needed, there would be fewer folks in the ER. Sadly, the current state of affairs leads to too many people who use the ER as their primary care clinic.

Ending the inefficient delivery of healthcare will save us money. It will cost us less than it does now. The Critics will be sad to see their lobbyist friends suffering and, therefore, will be kicking and screaming to prevent a sensible National Healthcare Program from being implemented. Don't be fooled by their protestations. Feel the relief in knowing your health will be in better hands. We already pay for it.

67. Moderation in Moderation

Engaging younger voters will take more than running a candidate who appeals as a moderate. Some of you may have noticed the Republicans have left moderation behind already. The modern conservative candidates are extremely anti-government and are supported not just by business first ideologies, but fanatics who prefer white supremacism, anarchy, and are disinclined toward democracy.

Young people have been born into a political world full of vitriol and hate. They blame the older generation for screwing up the planet, not just the country. The status quo never did cut it. It has rumbled along in glacial fashion, eroding the foundations of the common welfare and taking down the Earth's environment along with it.

A fresher vision in how to proceed is needed to capture the hearts of new voters. A turn to the left is really a return to where the common good is first and foremost. A country where the monied interests aren't given priority over the needs of the citizens. We must move forward with a daring new approach to achieve a better society for all of us.

Inspiring young voters to turn out means giving them the belief that things can change for the better. We can improve the lives of our fellow citizens if we encourage them to vote. To get them to vote, we must provide hope. No one said Democracy would ever be easy, and it works best as a participation activity. It is well past time for true, positive change to occur.

The Conservative movement has demonstrated they have no interest in Democracy by removing people from voter rolls, gerrymandering real demographic representation out, and, worst of all, supporting a man who by all actions and words aspires to be our New Führer . Democracy is under attack in our country, and it can only be restored by getting everyone out to vote, while we still can.

This is no time for moderation; inspiration will come from fresh concepts on making this a better country for all. We've had forty years of "trickle nowhere" as money has been put into fewer and fewer hands. Business has been compromised by allowing ever larger corporate mergers and takeovers, stifling competition and the chances of smaller businesses to succeed.

Instilling a sense of imminent and positive change is the way to get everyone out to vote. Same old, same old won't inspire. People need to believe that health, income inequality, social security, infrastructure, and education issues can be addressed. Belief in positive change will get folks out to vote. The message of hope needs to rise above the din of negativity that permeates conservative "logic." Civilization in our time! It is achievable, maybe even without shouting.

So, let's not speak of moderation. Let's go forth with a vision enabling us to know a better world awaits us all. It's not science fiction. We can do this. We have the tools available to make this work. Working

towards a brighter future can inspire people to vote. Let's be inspiring.
Please vote for inspiration. Hope to vote.

68. It's Better to Be Active Than Radioactive
     – Popular Idiom

Working towards a carbon-free energy grid system has resurrected the consideration of nuclear power. The "cleanliness" of nuclear power has been touted as the reason to begin a new round of construction. Unfortunately, the only clean part about it is that it doesn't spew carbon dioxide. The downside is conveniently swept under the rug.

The extremely unclean part of nuclear power is the production of nuclear waste. Many people want to believe it gets encapsulated in glass and can then be safely disposed of. The sad fact is that this hasn't ever happened. The encapsulation part hasn't been perfected. "Permanent" disposal lacks a safe resting spot; it doesn't exist. Everywhere nuclear waste is created becomes a "temporary" storage location.

There was a site being created in Nevada for permanent "safe" burial, but it was abandoned for political reasons. After all, who wants this waste dumped in their backyard? There just aren't many folks out there begging to have this economic "windfall" placed in their state.

Currently, most nuclear waste is just being "temporarily" stored on site as it has been since the first reactor was built. Every state with a reactor has its own pile of slowly decaying hazardous waste. In Washington State, we've been on the federal government for over thirty years to properly clean up the Hanford Site, where the original Manhattan Project plutonium was produced over seventy years ago.

Nowhere in sight is there a way and place(s) where permanent, "safe" storage can be made. There is a simple reason for this. It costs a lot of money. If you factor in the cost of containment for nuclear energy in with its production cost, it will never compete with truly green energy sources like solar and wind.

But, wait, the story continues. One other drawback of nuclear power production is another environmental detriment. Lots of clean, cool water is needed to not only cool the rods, but to provide the steam to drive the generators. Reactors are always placed next to or on a river, sending warmer water downstream, upsetting natural ecosystems.

This brings the conversation to the final drawback—catastrophic failure, due to either human error or natural disaster. Who really wants their river or ocean to be compromised by nuclear effluent? Ask the Japanese. They're getting out of the business.

The true cost of nuclear power production, from generation to waste disposal to disaster cleanup, is never brought up by the proponents of nuclear power. If it was factored into the kilowatt hour cost, no one would ever think to undertake such a risky proposition. It is cost prohibitive.

The only ones who make money on reactors are the construction companies. The power company may also, until they file for bankruptcy and let the government pay for cleanup. We, the people, should stop paying for that. We haven't been able to cover costs on seventy years of nuclear waste, with no hope on the horizon as to when we might get it under control.

The Nuclear Power Industry hasn't taken on total cost of its energy production. If that had been accounted for way back when, we wouldn't have piled up the tons of waste we currently need to address. The power brokers expect us to cover their costs on that.

No more! Be active, stay green. Let's not make that mistake again. Nuclear waste is expensive garbage. Let's look towards the day when we've finished paying for it. Could that be in just a half-life?

69.   Plant the Seeds to Counteract Climate Change

One more shout out to the Trillion Tree Initiative. If you do the math on this, with seven billion on the planet, it comes out to only 140 trees each. This is very doable. Is it okay to use the term, very doable? The cost for doing this should just come out of our everyday expenses for gas and energy consumption. We should all contribute to bringing back the trees we've been cutting down for millennia.

Let's not let the "do-nothing" approach win, because that obviously accomplishes nothing. The concept of tree planting might seem too big for some folk to wrap their heads around. Making a planet-wide effort to directly affect climate change is perfectly natural. Recreating forests where they once thrived would be a fitting method to address excess carbon in the atmosphere.

We have, as a planet, been creating excess carbon since before the beginning of the industrial age in the 1800s. In the 1900s we doubled down on excess CO_2 time and again. It's about time we owned up. Now is the time for direct action. The math is already out that even if we stopped all carbon dioxide production today, the excess already created would take more than a hundred years to dissipate.

The best way to gobble up all that CO_2 is to have trees out there doing the work. Once the trees have become forests, they will help to shift climate patterns that have contributed to the desertification of the planet. We can make positive change if we step up to the plate. This is not a pipe dream. It's the simplest and most direct way to work toward climate change reversal.

As for the Disbelievers of climate change, they will be the first to blame the government for not doing anything about it when Mar Al Lago falls into the sea. They should blame themselves for voting in people who believe Big Business profits should always trump ecological disaster. We do pay for the consequences of our actions.

In the long run, it's very cost effective. Coupled with clean energy projects we will make strides toward a carbon neutral future. It makes sense to pay for carbon clean up through levies on oil, gas. and coal. Pennies on the dollar go a long way toward reducing carbon dioxide. Small bites will help to achieve the goal without breaking the bank. There will be jobs!

70.   She Said, He Said

Any attempt at rational discussion undertaken with the modern conservative will invariably lead away from policy. They will fall back to their standard quips about spending money, government interfering with business, labeling such as Socialism or Liberal, migrants invading our borders, or Defending the Constitution.

Policy discussions erode into emotional statements that leave concrete solutions and defining platforms behind. This nebulous ground they stand on has no form or solid definition. Instead, they'll initiate attacks on their opposition, likely accusing the opposition of the very things of which they are most guilty of. Voter fraud, for instance, or ignoring the Constitution.

Meanwhile, legislation from the House keeps piling up, ignored, while the Republicans rant about the do-nothing Democrats. Doing nothing is the Republican standard; it doesn't cost them anything to do nothing. Doing nothing saves them from having to spend money doing Something. It's a happy place for them.

In the meantime, here's a small compilation of retorts for those who want to accomplish Something to quash the vacuous standard utterances of today's conservative. Afterwards, propose policy discussion, once again.

Conservative – Are you Capitalist or Socialist?

Reply – Which do you prefer, Socialism for the Rich or Democracy?

Con – How are you going to pay for National Healthcare?

Reply – Don't you want to see Americans save money on their healthcare?

Con – Raising the minimum wage is bad for Business!

Reply – All Americans deserve a living wage.

Con – How are you going to pay for Early Childhood Education?

Reply – All children need their best chance to achieve. For our country to continue leadership in innovation, education must be prioritized.

Con – Migrants are invading our borders!

Reply – Do you approve of separating children from their parents?

Con - Social Security needs to be privatized!

Reply – You want to take away this reliable income from those who have paid for it?

Con – Entitlements like Medicaid and Medicare are straining the Federal Budget!

Reply – You would take away these programs every American has paid into?

Con – Socialized Medicine!

Reply – All Americans should be able to save money on their healthcare.

Or Reply – Do you want Americans to have profits determine their health decisions?

Con – Entitlements need reducing to pay for infrastructure!

Reply –You're willing to allow vital water, road, and power distribution infrastructure to deteriorate?

71.   A Brief History of Early Millennium Events

Many newer voters don't have a first-hand recollection of events which occurred in the early years of the twenty-first century. The aughts were a time of historic events which have shaped our current state of affairs.

In 2000, for the first time in over one hundred years, a president was elected without the benefit of the popular vote. George W. Bush referred to this as a mandate to reimplement the trickle-down theory of taxation after years of the debt having been paid down. He started the deficit at two hundred billion dollars, and it's grown ever since, never less than three hundred billion dollars.

September 11, 2001 shocked us and the world as four passenger jets were used to destroy the World Trade Center Towers and smash into the Pentagon. We are still reeling from the chain of events this started. We'll get back to that.

The next month, Enron, a behemoth in the energy industry, began a flameout bigger than any business failure ever, $63.4 billion, at the time. Fraudulent accounting practices to boost stock prices led to eventual bankruptcy and the loss of thousands of workers' jobs and pensions. It would be many years before any of the perpetrators ever saw justice.

An alliance was formed to combat terrorism and the invasion of Afghanistan began in October, to root out Al-Qaeda and Osama bin

Laden. Afghanistan had already been embroiled in war, then civil war, since the 1979 invasion by the USSR. Suffering has been the daily life of its citizens ever since.

After the alliance forces swept through the country, George W. committed his greatest act of hubris. He was never happy with his dad for having left Iraq in the hands of Saddam Hussein. He decided he was going to go in and finish the job. Coming up with phony intel on the "stockpiles of weapons of mass destruction" which Saddam supposedly was keeping against international laws, W. got the international support he needed to invade Iraq, ultimately destabilizing the entire Mid-East.

The weapons of mass destruction? Never found. It was a complete fabrication, costing thousands of our lives, and hundreds of thousands of lives in Iraq, still ongoing. This act of hubris by W. led a coalition of international forces to invade a sovereign country for no legitimate reason. Will the Republicans ever own up to this being an actionable offence by one of its own? Nope. Not under current sub-standards.

Due to the lack of attention by the populace at large, W. was reelected. He did present an affable personality. Under his watch, though, even greater Big Business shenanigans were underway. W. said the banks would self-regulate themselves because they obviously wanted to stay in business. So much money was being made in the real estate market, bad loans became standard, and banks wanted to keep up with each other.

In 2007, it started unravelling. Banks and insurance companies were beginning another round of failures, much like they had during the Reagan and elder Bush years. In 2008, the largest bank failure ever, Washington Mutual, with over three hundred billion dollars in assets, was acquired by JP Morgan for $1.9 billion. I wish I had had a spare $1.9 billion, then. This pattern of shady business seems to follow the supply-side policies whenever enacted.

Also, in 2007 and 2008, with markets crumbling, the automobile manufacturers started going under. Then, massive government layoffs were instituted to counter the burgeoning deficit, further undermining the economy. Obama was elected and subsequently blamed for massive deficit spending while the government underwrote keeping banks, insurance, and auto companies afloat. Those hundreds of billions in loans were paid back, though, by and large.

Bank regulations were enacted. Safety mechanisms were put into place to keep these problems from recurring. Unfortunately, many of those regulations have been rescinded by the current administration as being too burdensome on Big Business. So, lots of homeowners were foreclosed on and lost their homes, that was in 2007. Many of these folks have never recovered. They still don't have homes or the equity they had invested in, despite current claims of a robust economy. They are a disaffected and angry group, whose needs should be addressed.

History has a nasty way of repeating itself. We are at a precipice where a giant U-turn needs to be made. We can no longer afford to have the foxes in charge of the hen house. Like Marshawn Lynch says, we've got to take care of our chickens. (I paraphrase there.) Let's vote out the foxes raiding our pocketbooks. They are only making the swamp murkier and more slippery. The swamp isn't being drained; our future is being mortgaged away from our children to concentrate the money into fewer hands.

Please, if you aren't already registered, get registered to vote. The bad money managers need to be removed from the government they don't believe in in the first place. The primrose path they continue to espouse only leads to less money for proper care of our country and people.

Register and use your vote to move us in positive directions! It's time to keep Big Money – and foreign influences - out of our elections. We the people have the power to vote in truly representative government. You must vote, to maintain your right to vote. Participate in Democracy; it's the only way to get your voice heard.

72. Present Tense

Yes, the present is very tense. The Party to End All Other Parties has gone all in. Voter suppression, gerrymandering, delisting registered voters, and now fully supporting The Tweeter-in-Chief, without admitting to his willingness to flout rules and the law to satisfy his personal whims. It is frightening they are willing to go so far to maintain party power, Democracy be damned.

Democracy is not their goal, just ultimate control. Currently sitting on hundreds of bills in the Senate which had been passed in the House, meanwhile referring to Democrats as Do-Nothing. All their greatest accusations are just pinpointing what they themselves are most guilty of. You can fool some of the people all the time; that is their strength.

You can't complain if you don't vote. You should complain vigorously if you have been prevented from voting. Don't let that happen again. Make sure you're registered. Leave work early if you have to or come in late. My previous employer had a policy of allowing a two-hour window for employees to vote, maybe your employer does, too.

We no longer need that two hours in Washington State because we've gone all in on mail-in ballots. Everyone can fill out their ballot in the comfort of their own home and send it off, postage paid! Think of the people hours saved if every state used this method. Staffing and supplying polling booths wouldn't be a burden, testing the organizational skills and resources of county governments the country over.

Participation should be easier. Who wants to go out into two feet of snow to get their ballot in? Well, do it if there is no other option, but weather shouldn't have to affect the outcome of elections. Novembers can be might unfriendly!

73.   A Free Press Under Duress

Fake News! Fake News! That's what the greatest perpetrators of fake news say the most and loudest. They revile the "Liberal Press" all the while making up stories. Meanwhile, the protections of a free press are whittled away as fewer companies control ever more media sources, including paper, TV, Radio, and Internet. Quality journalists are let go, allowing the popular Media Giant "news bureau," FOX News, to generate spin on political subjects pertinent to us all. It's unlikely you'll ever see a Pulitzer Prize awarded to FOX.

Separating quality in-depth news reporting from opinion-oriented, biased "news delivery" can be difficult to see. Add in all the unfiltered internet blather and trying to nail down the facts on actual events makes determining what is real and what is misrepresented harder than ever to do.

There are still a number of well-known news sources that continually try presenting the news accurately. Independent newspapers and associations still survive out there. They back up what they print, unlike the ghostwriters out on the ethernet. It is important for us to support the Free Press, as it is under great attack by the Tweeter-in-Chief, a consortium of Conservative Causes, and well-endowed Monied Interests.

Foreign Powers have invaded the popular culture internet, doing their very best to influence the perception of our government and spreading false rumors of about who will take our rights away. The ones who want to take our rights away have already shown themselves in states like Georgia, North and South Carolina, and Wisconsin. They are actively removing people from the voting rolls. The most basic right of all, being stripped away by the hundreds of thousands.

The fake news outlets try to discourage voters who would otherwise tend to vote Democratic by telling them that not voting will "stick it to the man" and show them you don't think you're being represented. It is hard to get represented if you don't vote. Voting is the single most important right Democracy has to offer. Don't let that right wither on the vine.

The Free Press is attacked for standing up to an administration which is one by one dismantling environmental, health, and job safety protections. These protections were put into place for us. Removing them might save a few dollars for a given corporation, but it won't benefit us. Those protections were providing jobs, taking care of our health and properly looking after the environment.

In taking a stand against this intolerant administration, the Free Press is accused of undermining government and threatening due process, when the opposite is the truth. We are in alarming times regarding the state of the Free Press. He-Who-Would-Be-King has said he'd like to start a "government run" news organization! That would be a direct take down of the Constitution's First Amendment.

Please support a Free Press by buying a local paper that presents news stories without editorializing everything. Share your thoughts and insights with friends. Make use of relevant information to make informed decisions. This current Age of Misinformation must be brought back to fact. It's okay to question something and get a second source to verify it. Just be sure the source is reputable. Get verification of the facts before initiating another tweetstorm.

74.   The Deep State of Mind

In a completely related way, "The Deep State" has continued to undermine the Free Press and Democracy. Amongst all the conspiracy
theories, the one that the government is behind any number of nefar-
ious acts aimed at taking total control of our lives conveniently shoves
aside that the real conspiracy out there is to undermine a true Free
Press and replace Democracy with a singular new Führer who is de-
lighted to accede to this lofty perch which he sees as his birthright—
Trump Forever. He has arrived at the right time and place for the total
power grab, with a multitude of minions crowding around trying to
win his temporary approval.

Temporary is the catch word here as Trump considers himself perfect in every way, and the rest of us will just never measure up. If you
are not fawning over His Grace, you're not worthy of his attention. His
Trumpeters are now all in. Opposing Trump is tantamount to sedition!
Denying him his whims, treachery! Undermining his desires is now a
declamation deserving of death!

This Emperor's robes need removing.

For all you Deep State conspiracy theorist fans out there, follow
the money. It's not the Deep State, it's the Deep Pockets that are funding the conspiracy. It has worsened since the passage of the Citizens
United decision allowing Big Money to be thrown around to dissuade

you from voting for people who would rather not have us ruled by the privileged elite. Remember, we had a revolution to throw off the House of Lords.

We the People still have a chance to regain the reins of government. It starts with recognizing the right to vote must be utilized every year. Not once, but twice, every year, primary and general election. Voting is the fundamental right that is currently most endangered. The Party to End All Parties really isn't interested in Democracy; it interferes with their desire to control. That has become more and more obvious.

Government by the people, for the people, that's what's written of in the Declaration of Independence. Vote for the people. Vote for people who believe that government is not the problem but that letting the Moneyed Interests control government is. Big Money will never need government assistance; they're big already.

It's said that just in the US there are over six hundred billionaires. Our upcoming fiscal deficit is expected to be one trillion dollars. That's one thousand billions. Hmmm, maybe each billionaire could spot a billion; that would get us closer to closing that gap. Would that make them homeless? Would they not be able to feed their families? It's food for thought!

How did we get to this Deep State of Mind where a megalomaniac is in charge, unfettered, with minions who are willing to ignore excesses of power? It boggles the mind! The world's once premier Democracy is on the precipice of falling under the heavy hand of one human who believes he can do no wrong. With a willing cadre of elected supporters ready to countenance any whim, he smites his enemies for any perceived deviation from total devotion.

Complacency created this situation. Apathy allowed it to take hold. By not voting, people encouraged this deep state of impending democratic implosion. It is time to return the government into the hands of the people. Getting greater turnouts at the polls is the only way to bring about positive change to the day to day operation of the National Government.

Republicans have revealed themselves as not interested in Democracy, just total control. GOP now stands for Greedy Old Patriarchs. For positive change we need positive people, not those who preach divisiveness and fear. We need more people to buy into Democracy to make it work for everyone, not just the 1 percent. What it will take is getting people off their duff twice a year to make a positive difference for our lives. Put down your cell phones twice a year to get out and vote. Participate!

Do you want to piss off the Deep State? Get the Deep Pockets out of our government. Vote out the Money Lords. Let's get this right from now on. Participate in empowering the 99 percent. The Monied Interests will never make it right. We, the 99 percent, must wrest back control while we still can. Voting is the only way to accomplish this. Vote out those who are ruled by Big Money. Please! Do it this year! Do it every year!

It can and will get better. Exercise your right to vote. Twice a year. Get out there and participate with your fellow citizens. It'll feel great in the long run. Ninety-nine percent of us are counting on you. Get your peeps out there with you. It's the most important exercise you ever do.

75.　A Living Document

There are a lot of folks out there who claim to be Constitutionalists. As if it was intended to never receive any updating. It is not the Ten Commandments. It is not chiseled in stone. It was intended to be a framework for Democracy, subject to change as times changed. Like TJ said, we can't let our barbarous ancestors' control how we vote today.

Democracy is dependent on majority rule. We are seeing Republicans doing whatever they can to maintain their control, majority be damned. Gerrymandering districts to produce super majority Republican representation in states where it just does not exist. Democracy is not in their wheelhouse.

The courts are being stacked in their favor, allowing these unrepresentative districts to remain in force, despite statewide misrepresentations. Democracy is under attack.

The Constitution was created as a living document. For those of you who have kept a copy in your pocket to show your support for it, I remind you it has been amended over twenty times. It is subject to majority rule, subject to the will of the people, subject to change.

It has become ever more obvious it needs further improvement. While the Party of Anti-Democracy can wield its power, positive change will be impossible to attain. Complacency over many years has led to a lack of participation in Democracy. The time to believe in the power of the vote is now. To make Democracy work for the majority, the majority must vote.

If we can get at least 85 percent of folk voting twice a year, we can make Democracy work for all of us. Complacency over the years has led to infrastructure failure. It has undermined Democracy. We are in danger of losing our power to vote.

There are signs that increasing numbers of people are registering to vote; that's good. If you have been paying attention, you know there are "leaders" who wish to summarily implement their will upon the people. They denounce those who dissent—a first amendment right—as treason. There is no time like the present to vote in representatives who want Democracy.

The vote is the cornerstone of Democracy. Let's encourage it with deductions on our taxes for primary and general elections. Five hundred dollars for each one should help provide incentive. Complacency has allowed the forces of Anti-Democracy to promote a One-Party system. The 99 percent can make themselves heard.

As a living document, the Constitution can be made to ensure that the majority of people are represented. It will take participation. Get out there and be counted. Together we can make this work for all of us. Vote to preserve Democracy. Vote at least twice a year. We can make a positive difference.

76. Focus Up!

Back to Chapter One. The Democrats need to present their platform simply. People aren't interested in all the details, that's why we have elected representatives out there to hammer out the finer points. Those who would just have future generations pay for their mistakes will always complain about costs, but never own up to any responsibility. So…

Legislating the Citizens United out of our lives is paramount. Big Money must be removed from influencing government. There is no place for that in government by the people.

National Healthcare needs to become a reality. It's not how much it will cost, it's the six hundred billion dollars (round figure—or probably more!) we'll save by self-insuring ourselves. The big companies are already doing this; let's just be a single force of three hundred million, able to negotiate fair and affordable services and prescriptions for everyone. Make it better than Medicare!

Bringing the minimum wage to fifteen dollars per hour, with built-in cost of living raises, will work to get wage inequality under to control. Raising the minimum wage is the only way to get wage inequality addressed. It will help get people off the streets and public assistance.

Shoring up Social Security is a must. This safety net for retirement can be properly addressed without reductions in payments for those who have put a lifetime of sweat into the system. Don't call it an Entitlement! We have worked for this; dang it, we earned it!

Education, especially early education, must be provided to keep us ahead in this increasingly fast-paced world. It can end inherited poverty. We can't maintain our advanced lifestyle without staying ahead in innovation and research.

Infrastructure must be properly addressed. We can't cut corners on our water supplies, roads, or energy production and distribution. These are essential factors in day-to-day life which require investment and maintenance. They can't be allowed to fail. Infrastructure provides quality jobs.

So...The above six items are it in a nutshell. The economy has been humming along for a decade now; there is plenty of money here to be able to address these needs without increasing our collective debt. Good Government is necessary to get our infrastructure properly taken care of. The Anti-Government crowd will never run Government with fiscal responsibility in mind.

Focusing up on these six simple concepts can get us to move forward. The rest is white noise to distract us from the most important issues which need addressing. Stick with these basics. People will get behind well spent dollars. It's cheaper to maintain infrastructure than it is to fix it when it falls apart.

Keep it simple. Emphasize fiscal responsibility. Emphasize how it saves money. "A stitch in time saves nine." It's so true! All of us need to contribute in some way. Our society and civilization require Interdependence. We are not all islands out there; we are interdependent on each other to get through every day. Taking care of all of the above will make it work for everyone.

The devil is in the details, but details are not necessary on the campaign trail. Stay on point with our common goals, which are to better the situation for us in the 99 percent. The common good must be the message. Keep it simple, focus on that.

77.   Coronavirus Addition

As if there weren't already enough issues to address, pandemic strikes. In just the last twenty years we've had SARS, MERS, Swine Flu, and Ebola to contend with. More than the previous one hundred years. Did anyone think the odds were that it couldn't happen again? Apparently, yes.

We've been caught with our pants down, and the only way to pull them up will be with greater testing. The lack of a cohesive centralized approach has been mind-bogglingly thrown out the window to keep the true numbers of affected from imposing themselves on our collective psyche. It may help dissuade a bit of hysteria, but it won't get the job completed.

Waiting for someone to shows signs of infection before allowing them to take a test is no way to get a grip on a highly transmittable disease. Aggressive testing, following the path of the infected moving through the populace, as is done with STDs, is the only way to staunch the epidemic.

Unfortunately, our Narcissist-in-Chief believes higher numbers will lower his esteem among the kingdom's populace. We will never know how many were infected, died from, or who may have acquired immunity (if that is possible) since the disease has been allowed to go unchecked since January. Actual numbers are now impossible. Only aggressive, reliable testing will get us to the end of this plague.

Development of reliable tests for the above has been stymied by direction at the top. The buck definitely stopped at the desk of Donald the First and he blew it off. Only good, unfettered testing will see us to the end of this coronavirus. The lack of belief in applied science has hindered the encapsulation of Covid-19.

Aggressive testing will get us through this morass. Properly funding the CDC will enable the scientists, researchers, and medical professionals to get their arms around this pandemic and the future diseases which are sure to sprout up. Pointing fingers and assigning blame won't get anywhere. Taking action will get us to resolution.

Covid-19 is a wakeup call for us. It has unveiled one of the problems with our current healthcare approach. People have lost their jobs and insurance! This is no way to protect us from the ravages of epidemic episodes.

Politics has been blamed for a lack of progress in getting help out. The ones blaming politics are the ones most responsible for no cohesive process to get this coronavirus under control or provide for the many now suffering economically from the consequences.

It has been suggested that since Corporations are now considered people, we could give each of them $1,200, also. Along those lines, we will have to make sure that no one loses their home over this. No banks should foreclose on anyone because the repercussions from social distancing has kept people from earning a paycheck. We don't need a repeat of 2008.

It has been sobering to see how circumstances can change is such a short period of time. Together, we can make it through this. With resolve, we can move forward from this. With willpower, we will get through it and be stronger on the other side. Let's stand together—six feet apart—demonstrating strength and unity, knowing we will get through this by working together.

Et al.) Further Rumblings

Black Lives Do Matter! Please let this recurring nightmare end!

Greater mileage could be achieved with all current cars if a full-time display, available for all passengers to see, of the current actual fuel use in Miles Per Gallon. It would be like a game; try to see the highest score you can get!

I was supposed to write this over five years ago. Therefore, I take full responsibility for the debacle the 2016 election became. Yes, it was all my fault. Now you know.

Your home purchase is the greatest investment you will probably ever make. Treat it like an investment, not an ATM; unless you're using it for home improvement, that is what refinancing is for. The banks will try to make you think you should tap into it for anything; that lead to the collapse of 2008. After you're forty, you should think about paying it off as soon as possible—time for a fifteen-year mortgage. That's what will get you to retirement sooner with greater security and peace of mind.

Even if you are one of the lucky ones to be working in a job that includes an actual pension, putting money aside in 401ks and other Tax-Sheltered Annuities (TSA) is a great way to prepare for life after work.

In my working days, I was able to borrow from my TSA to purchase a car. This is essentially paying yourself the interest for the loan. What a great way to borrow! Not all plans have that option, but it's worth looking into.

Should this book sell like hotcakes, I will put money towards voter registration drives in Georgia, North Carolina, and Wisconsin—as a start.

Believe in love. Conquering hate is a monumental task, but worth the effort. Keep the faith! Most people really do want equality, justice and fairly distributed outcomes. Give hope.

Fear is a paralyzer. Keep its grip off you. Look for solutions. Make lemonade.

Listen. Allow yourself to be heard. Take a breath to listen again. If you can't get a word in edgewise on a rant, walk away.

Stay positive, you are not alone; there are many who want positive change and equitable outcomes.

Donate to food banks if you can; there is much inequity out there.

Every day try to make the world a better place, however incremental it may seem.

Hugs are free, though, in trying times, elbow bumps might have to do.

Smiles are contagious, infect someone today.